AF600553

COMMON LAW MARRIAGE

THE CATHOLIC UNIVERSITY OF AMERICA
CANON LAW STUDIES
No. 153

COMMON LAW MARRIAGE

BY

Robert E. Dillon, A.B., J.C.L.

Priest of the Diocese of Syracuse

A DISSERTATION

Submitted to the Faculty of Canon Law of the Catholic University of America in Partial Fulfillment of the Requirements for the Degree of Doctor of Canon Law

THE CATHOLIC UNIVERSITY OF AMERICA PRESS
WASHINGTON, D. C.
1942

NIHIL OBSTAT:

Hieronymus D. Hannan, S.T.D., J.C.D.
Censor Deputatus.

Washingtonii, D. C., die 22 Maii, 1942.

IMPRIMATUR:

✠Gualterus A. Foery, D.D.
Episcopus Syracusensis.
Syracusis, die 25 Maii, 1942.

MURRAY & HEISTER, WASHINGTON, D. C.
Printed in the United States of America

TABLE OF CONTENTS

INTRODUCTION

THE custody of the true doctrine of marriage is at once one of the highest honors and one of the most solemn obligations of the Catholic Church. That it is an honor to teach mankind the dignity of the marital union, to guide man to the fulfillment of the God-given obligations of that union, and to protect that union from the encroachments of false teaching and sinful practice, no one can deny. That it is the obligation of the Church to perpetuate the true doctrine of marriage is apparent from the commission of her Divine Founder to teach all nations "to observe all things whatsoever I have commanded you." [1]

By its divine institution at the beginning of human history, marriage has been declared indissoluble. Old Testament history proves how manifold were the vices and how great the ignominies heaped upon this solemn union by heathens, and even by the Chosen Race. But as our late Holy Father, Leo XIII, clearly and beautifully declared, marriage was recalled from its degraded state:

"Jesus Christ, who restored our human dignity and who perfected the Mosaic law, applied early in His ministry no little solicitude to the question of marriage. He ennobled the marriage in Cana of Galilee by His presence, and made it memorable by the first of miracles which He wrought; and for this reason, even from that day forth, it seemed as if the beginnings of new holiness had been conferred on human marriage." [2]

---

[1] Matt. XXVIII: 19, 20.

[2] Encyclical Letter, *Arcanum Divinae,* Feb. 10, 1880—*Codicis Iuris Canonici Fontes cura Emi. Petri Card. Gasparri Editi* (9 vols. Romae [postea Civitate Vaticana]: Typis Polyglottis Vaticanis, 1923-39, Vols. VII–IX ed. cura et studio Emi. Iustiniani Card. Serédi), n. 580. (Hereafter this work will be cited *Fontes.*) English translation from *The Great Encyclical Letters of Pope Leo XIII* (New York, Cincinnati, Chicago: Benziger Bros., 1903), p. 62.

But the custody of the doctrine of marriage has not always been conceded to the Church. Civil rulers have sought to deprive marriage of its holiness, and so to bring it into the sphere of those rights which, instituted by man, are ruled and administered solely by the civil jurisprudence of man. Common law marriage, as practiced in many of the United States of America, affords a striking example of the confusion resulting from the usurpation of rightly constituted authority. Uncertainty, confusion and lack of clarity abound when a common law marriage affords the basis of judicial discussion.

In an endeavor to present the teaching of the Catholic Church on common law marriage, the present work endeavors to show whether or not a common law marriage could or did exist under the laws of the Church prior to the promulgation of the new Code of Canon Law in 1918, and whether or not a common law marriage may lawfully exist under the present legal system of the Church. Consideration has also been given to some of the procedural problems which confront the judicial treatment of common law marriage, as well as to the attitude of the penal law of the Church towards this institution. The canonical viewpoint, not the view of a civil lawyer, has been adopted throughout, though at times it has been necessary to summarize, within the limited capability of the writer, the civil law viewpoint of common law marriage.

The writer wishes to express his sincere gratitude to His Excellency, the Most Reverend Walter A. Foery, Bishop of Syracuse, for the opportunity of graduate study, to the members of the Faculty of the School of Canon Law of the Catholic University of America for their kind assistance and guidance in the preparation of this work, and to many others, especially the student priests at the Catholic University of America, for their generous assistance.

CHAPTER I

Marriage at American Common Law

Article 1. What is the Common Law?

The term common law is herein used to signify a customary law adopted by the peoples of England and the United States and accepted by them as having a certain undefined binding force. It is not the same as the *Ius Gentium* which obtained in the Roman legal system to govern the business transactions of citizens and foreigners (*peregrini*) until such time as the latter became naturalized Roman citizens; this *Ius Gentium* later merged with the Roman *Ius Civile* (which was exclusively for Roman citizens) to form one system. During the greater part of the legal history of mankind, most nations have had a single legal system as their standard for the government of their citizens.

The law of the United States, however, apart from constitutions and treaties, is twofold: statutory law and common law. As its name implies, statutory law comprises those enactments which emanate from legislative bodies, whether federal, state or municipal. It is also called enacted law.[1]

Common law, on the contrary, is not the result of positive action by the lawmakers of the country, except that common law was adopted by statute in all the states, but is rather the universal concept of law which tradition has formed. Called many times the " unwritten law," it exists unseen as do many customary social and ethical norms. As a beacon it directs legislators in their formation of statute law. So too, it shows the way whereby judges must proceed in administering justice, and in applying statutory law to particular cases. The courts of the land, in adjudicating cases according to their understanding of the common law, have crystallized its form to a great degree, so that the juris-

[1] Smith, *Handbook of Elementary Law,* Hornbook Series (2 ed., St. Paul, Minn.: West Publishing Co., 1939), p. 50.

prudence of the country gives a fairly accurate synopsis of the common law. Thus, for the lawyer, the system of common law is defined by Dean Roscoe Pound of the Harvard Law School as: "the body of received materials in which those who decide cases are held and hold themselves bound to find the grounds of decision." [2]

Because the common law of the United States rests on principles derived from the common law of England,[3] it will be advisable here to inspect briefly the English common law in so far as it affects marriage at American common law.

In England, the customs of the Mercian law, Wessex law, and Danish law prevailed until the Norman conquest of 1066. From that time on, the centralization of governmental powers effected a uniformity of legal customs, which during the reign of King Edward I (1272–1307), became known as the common law.[4] The basis of matrimonial law, however, in England, as throughout Europe, was the Canon Law of the Church.[5]

Prior to the Norman conquest, civil and ecclesiastical courts in England were not separated, and the distinction between their jurisdictions was vague. On the bench, which tries both civil and ecclesiastical breaches of law, sat secular and ecclesiastical officials side by side. The bishop was included on the bench by virtue of his office. Though William the Conqueror instituted a definition between the ecclesiastical courts and those of secular justice, and though immediately after this change the ecclesiastical courts do not seem to have insisted too strongly on their claim that marriage belonged to their exclusive jurisdiction, yet before the middle of the twelfth century marriage was completely turned over to Church courts for adjudication.[6] Cases concerning the bond of validity of marriage were tried in the ecclesiastical courts. If a case concerning the marriage bond or legitimacy of children

---

[2] Pound, Roscoe, "What is the Common Law?"—*Univ. of Chicago Review,* IV (1936–37), 176–189, esp. 179.

[3] Bucher v. Cheshire R. Co.—125 U. S. 555.

[4] Smith, *Handbook of Elementary Law,* p. 50.

[5] Dalrymple v. Dalrymple, 161 Eng. Rep. 665.

[6] Joyce, *Christian Marriage,* Heythrop Series: I (London and New York: Sheed and Ward, 1933), pp. 227, 228.

arose as an incidental case in the course of a trial in the temporal courts, it was remanded to the bishop and his court for adjudication. The temporal court abided by the bishop's decision in settling its case.[7]

This reservation to ecclesiastical courts of marriage adjudication made complete the Church's control of marriage. Her Canon law was the law of marriage; her court decisions were the application and interpretation of that law. Even though the Protestant Reformation attempted to abolish the direct influence of the Church, the legal heritage of centuries could not be disavowed over night. When the Catholic religion was proscribed in England, her Canon law and her courts lost legal recognition. Yet the common law preserved the Church law of marriage in many respects, and marriage cases, instead of being taken over by civil courts, were treated in Anglican Church courts. In one of the most outstanding decisions of these courts, it was ruled that those rules of Canon law which had their foundation in the natural and civil contract of marriage were retained.[8] Another decision had previously denied the Sacramental nature of Christian marriage.[9]

The common law of marriage then, in so far as it respects marriage, was that received from the Catholic Church in the eleventh century. Until the sixteenth century the common law of marriage was administered by the Church; and even when the law of England proscribed Catholicism, the Catholic principles of marriage which formed the basis of legislative and judicial procedure were retained.[10]

The decrees of the Council of Trent were not received in Eng-

---

[7] Pollock and Maitland, *History of English Law* (2 vols., Cambridge [Eng.] and Boston, 1895), II, 363.

[8] Dalrymple v. Dalrymple, 161 Eng. Rep. 665.

[9] Beamish v. Beamish, 11 Eng. Rep. 735.

[10] Cf. Joyce, *Christian Marriage*, p. viii.

Koegel, in his book *Common Law Marriage and Its Development in the United States* (Washington: John Byrne & Co., 1922), states on p. 15: "In any discussion of marriage at common law we must remember that in England the jurisdiction over marriage was divided between the spiritual and temporal tribunals, administering the canon and common law, respectively." This would seem to imply that common law marriage was outside the

land;[11] the status of common law marriage remained unchanged by the *Tametsi* decree.

In 1540, the English Parliament passed an act which provided that an unconsummated pre-contract should have no force against a subsequent marriage, celebrated ecclesiastically and consummated, but this act was shortly thereafter repealed, and common law marriage resumed its former status of validity,[12] which it retained until the Marriage Act of 1753, introduced by Lord Chancellor Hartwicke and passed by both Houses, Lords and Commons. By this Act common law marriages were rendered invalid in the future.[13]

Such was the status of common law marriage in England when the American colonists established their independence. Constrained by hereditary training, early American legalists had naught to rely upon as a basis for law except that system which had trained and protected them, and finally antagonized them. English common law and statutory law were received favorably by the early American colonists to the extent dictated by their position as protestants against the Mother Country and founders of the new nation. American courts have declared that the common law of the United States rests on principles derived from the common law of England,[14] though it is not the same as that of England.[15]

Some states accepted the common and statutory law of England as it existed during the " fourth year of the reign of James I," i.e. 1607, the date of the founding of the first perma-

---

province of ecclesiastical courts. But a further reading of the same page shows that the text he quotes in proof maintains that whatever pertained in marriage " to the capacity for contracting . . . the mode of contracting . . . and to its dissolution, complete or partial, belonged to the canon or ecclesiastical law and was administered by the spiritual courts. So much of it as affected the property rights . . . belonged to the common law and was administered in the temporal courts."

[11] Vermeersch-Creusen, *Epitome Iuris Canonici* (3 vols., Vol. I, 6 ed., 1937; Vols. II–III, 5 ed., 1936; Mechliniae-Romae: H. Dessain), II, n. 385, §3.

[12] Joyce, *Christian Marriage,* 137.

[13] Koegel, *Common Law Marriage,* pp. 29, 33.

[14] Bucher v. Cheshire R. Co., 125 U. S. 555.

[15] Van Ness v. Packard, 2 Pet. 137.

nent English colony in America. Other states accepted the English common law, and the statutes of that country enacted up to the date of the signing of the American Declaration of Independence, July 4, 1776. Still other some states set no date by which it might be determined when English statutory law ceased to find favor. But all states, except Louisiana, adopted it.[16]

Thus every state in the Union may have its local usages, customs, and common law, which common law may be determined in each state from its general policy, the usages sanctioned by its courts, and its statutes.[17] Finally, it is within the power of each state to change the common law of the state as it sees fit.[18]

ARTICLE 2. MARRIAGE AT AMERICAN COMMON LAW

The usual method of marriage in the United States is the formal, or ceremonial marriage. All the states set forth in their statutes a series of steps, which, if taken by a man and woman competent to marry, make them husband and wife. This course of procedure usually includes the procuring of a license, a device intended to prevent clandestine marriages, and to offer to persons cognizant of existing impediments an opportunity to make them known. Furthermore, the official issuing the license may require of the parties information pertinent to their state in life, so that he may determine their legal capability of entering the marriage contract.[19]

Once the license is secured, or public intention to marry is given in some other prescribed manner, the parties go to some officer, a priest, minister of the gospel, judge, justice of the peace, or civil magistrate; and if, in his presence, they express their agreement to become man and wife, he is authorized to pronounce them such. Some states usually require other witnesses for the

---

[16] Smith, *Handbook of Elementary Law,* p. 51.

Louisiana, having the Napoleonic Code as the basis of its law, does not have the English system of common law.

[17] Wheeler v. Smith, 9 How. 55.

[18] B. & O. R. R. v. Baugh, 149 U. S. 368.

[19] Madden, *A Handbook of the Law of Persons and Domestic Relations* (2 ed., St. Paul, Minn.: West Publishing Co., 1931), pp. 48, 49; May, *Marriage Laws and Decisions in the United States* (New York City: Russell Sage Foundation, 1929), pp. 15–20.

ceremony. In most cases the person solemnizing the marriage is required to return a certificate of that fact, viz., that he has married this couple, to a public officer, who is required by law to keep public record thereof, and to furnish proof to the parties of their marriage.[20]

Common law marriage, however, is one contracted without fulfillment of the statutory solemnities for marriage. "All that is required for a valid 'common law marriage' is that marriageable parties take each other as husband and wife, their intent and consent being declared by words, or even by letter. But only words in the present tense have this effect. A present intention to be husband and wife at some future time is ineffective, however expressed. The consent can only be *per verba de praesenti.* The rule that consent given *per verba de futuro cum copula* constitutes marriage does not affect the principle, for it is a rule of evidence by which parties are presumed to have converted their future promises into an actual marriage." [21]

The doctrine handed down by the Supreme Court of the United States is expressed in the words of Justice J. Strong: "That such a contract (*per verba de praesenti*) constitutes a marriage at common law there can be no doubt, in view of the adjudications made in this country, *from its earliest settlement to the present day.*" [22]

In civil law, the term "marriage" is taken to mean the civil contract between persons of opposite sex to become man and wife, or to mean the legal status ensuing from, and consequent upon, such a contract.[23] In several cases, the establishment of the

---

[20] Madden, *loc. cit.*

[21] Dept. of Commerce and Labor, *Special Reports: Marriage and Divorce* (2 vols., Washington: U. S. Gov't. Printing Office, 1909), I, p. 184. Cf. also Koegel, *Common Law Marriage*, pp. 138–140, wherein several cases and authors are cited in proof.

[22] Meister v. Moore, 96 U. S. 76. (Italics inserted by the writer.) In his book, Koegel questions the italicized words in this decision, and shows that in colonial days, the various colonies were against such marriages—*op. cit.*, pp. 55–75. However, as will be shown later, statutes against marriage do not invalidate such marriages, unless the law expressly, or equivalently, determines such nullity.

[23] May, *Marriage Laws and Decisions in the U. S.*, p. 7.

"status" as man and wife was sufficient to prove the validity of a common law marriage. In the famous Erlanger case in New York State, though a common law marriage was against the law at the time this marriage had been entered, the status perdured after the law ceased to exist, and the woman in the case was recognized as the legal widow of the deceased Mr. Erlanger.[24]

This distinction of civil law between the contract and the status of marriage corresponds to the canonical distinction between "*matrimonium in fieri*" and "*matrimonio in facto.*" Since, however, the common law marriage contract at the time of its inception usually lacks witnesses, or written testimony probative of its existence, the status of common law marriage is taken as presumptive of the existence of the contract. In some states, cohabitation is required for a valid informal contract of marriage, while in other states, neither cohabitation nor consummation is required.[25]

In a state recognizing common law marriage, and sometimes in a state not recognizing it, the general rule is that when parties have attempted a formal marriage, which fails because of some impediment, the continued cohabitation of the parties after the removal of the impediment constitutes a valid common law marriage.[26] If a state, either by its statute law or its jurisprudence, admits that a marriage is thus validated, no renewal or new exchange of consent is required; the mere continuation of their cohabitation suffices. But if the union was a meretricious one in

[24] O'Brien, *Common Law Marriage Status—Erlanger Opinion* (New York, 1932). This book reprints the testimony of the case "In the matter of the Estate of Abraham L. Erlanger, Deceased," tried in the Surrogate's Court, New York County, and recorded in *The Miscellaneous Reports of the State of N. Y.*, August, 1932. Cf. also Travers v. Reinhart, 205 U. S. 423.

[25] *In re Medford's Estate* (Supreme Court of Iowa), 196 N. W. 728, holding for the necessity of cohabitation. Murphy v. Ramsey, 114 U. S. 42; Davis v. Stouffer, 112 S. W. 262, which declare cohabitation not necessary. Cf. other cases cited in McCurdy, *Cases in the Law of Persons and Domestic Relations* (2 ed., National Case Book Series, Chicago: Callaghan and Co., 1933), p. 33.

[26] Travers v. Reinhart, 205 U. S. 423; Koegel, *Common Law Marriage*, 153-160; cf. also Alford, *Jus Matrimoniale Comparatum* (Roma: Anonima Libraria Cattolica Italiana, 1938), p. 291.

its inception, some courts have held that the continuance of cohabitation after the removal of the impediment does not constitute marriage. However if the union was only objectively a meretricious one and if the parties desired marriage and did everything in their power to effect it (for example, they entered a marriage agreement or solemnized marriage), then the courts are more inclined to consider such a union validated by the mere continuance of cohabitation once the impediment to marriage ceases. Court decisions are far from consonant in their settlement of these cases.[27]

A further question is presented whenever a man and woman who live together in a void ceremonial marriage in a state which does not recognize common law marriage move to a state in which it is recognized without in any way evidencing their intent to create a valid common law marriage. Does their presence in the state which recognizes common law marriage constitute a marriage, and if so, how long must they cohabit in such a state to create a common law marriage? Koegel, who proposes this question, shows the divergent opinions taken by courts in deciding cases of this nature.[28] He rightly concludes:

"This phase of the subject is in a hopeless condition.

[27] Koegel, *Common Law Marriage,* 153–155; this author cites the case wherein a valid common law marriage was declared between a white man and a colored woman who had moved from Alabama, a state which declares such marriages criminal, to Ohio (Johnson v. Dudley, 3 Ohio N. P. 196). Cf. also Hannan, "Automatic Sanation of Marriage."—*The Jurist* (Washington, D. C.: School of Canon Law, Catholic University of America, 1941–), I (1941), 146–149.

[28] *Op. cit.,* 156–160. In one case, Travers v. Reinhart (205 U. S. 423), a couple had entered a void ceremonial marriage in Virginia; some time later they moved to Maryland where they lived for fifteen years; neither Virginia nor Maryland recognized common law marriage; the couple then moved to New Jersey where, after six months residence, the man died; the court in New Jersey, a state which recognized common law marriage at that time, held that the couple were validly married. On the other hand, the Supreme Court of Massachusetts held (in Norcross v. Norcross, 155 Mass. 425) that the cohabitation for a short time in New York of persons, who were domiciled in Massachusetts and who were living together in an illegal union, did not constitute a common law marriage valid in New York and consequently accepted as valid in Massachusetts.

On principle the time element should not enter into the question. The rule is that if the parties enter into what by the law of the place is a marriage, whether they be there transiently or permanently, they are married. Therefore, if the mere continued cohabitation after the removal of an impediment to a valid ceremonial marriage constitutes a valid common law marriage, it would seem that if the parties desire and intend matrimony and merely pass through a jurisdiction recognizing common law marriage, a valid common law marriage would be created by the mere fact that they went through such a jurisdiction, even perhaps on a sleeping car, without ever knowing it." [29]

Statutes of various states may often militate against common law marriages without invalidating them. For unless statutes expressly nullify informal marriages, the laws are to be considered as only directory and not mandatory, i.e., creating prohibitive but not diriment impediments to such marriages. For civil law presumes the continuance of a right at common law until such time as that right be expressly and decidedly restricted by statute.[30] " No doubt, a statute may take away a common law right; but there is always a presumption that the legislature has no such intention, unless it is plainly expressed. A statute may declare that no marriages shall be valid unless they are solemnized in a prescribed manner; but such an enactment is a very different law from a law requiring all marriages to be entered into in the presence of a magistrate or clergyman, or that it be preceded by a license, or publication of the banns, or attested by witnesses. Such formal provisions may be construed as merely directory, instead of being treated as destructive of a common law right to form the marriage relation by words of present assent. And such, we think, has been the rule generally adopted in construing statutes regarding marriage." [31]

Common law marriage, then, is one entered into without the observance of statutory formalities, or the formalities prescribed

---

[29] *Ibid.*, p. 160.

[30] Madden, *A Handbook of the Law of Persons and Domestic Relations*, p. 47.

[31] Words of Justice J. Strong of the Supreme Court of the United States, in the case of Meister v. Moore (1877), 96 U. S. 76.

by religion. It is one entered into with consent of marriageable parties *per verba de praesenti,* since whenever the form *per verba de futuro cum copula* has been legally recognized as valid, the *copula* itself has been considered as constituting a present consent to marriage.[32]

ARTICLE 3. RECOGNITION OF COMMON LAW MARRIAGE IN THE UNITED STATES TODAY

Due to the independence with which each state wields legislative and judicial control over the marriages contracted within its jurisdiction, no general rule can be laid down by which the validity or nullity of a common law marriage in the United States can be determined. The laws of the particular states in which the marriage was contracted and in which the parties lived or appeared together as man and wife must be scrutinized. When the statute law of a state is silent concerning common law marriage, the presumption is that the right of the parties to marry at common law still persists; but many times the judicial decisions step in to declare that such a right no longer exists in that state. Furthermore, although a state may declare invalid any common law marriage contracted within its jurisdiction, the same state may and many times does recognize as valid those common law marriages which are contracted elsewhere, provided that, when contracted, the marriage was valid according to the law of the state in which it was contracted.

The following table lists the states and extra-territorial possessions of the United States which, as of December 31, 1941, recognize a common law marriage as valid: [33]

Alabama—(194 Ala. 613).
Alaska—(5 Alaska 107).
Colorado—
District of Columbia—(60 App. D.C. 218).
Florida—(63 So. 726).
Georgia—(30 Ga. 173).

[32] Cf. *supra,* p. 6; May, *Marriage Laws and Decisions in the U. S.,* p. 11.

[33] This list is compiled from references and quotations in *The Martindale-Hubbell Law Dictionary* (74th annual edition, 2 vols., Summitt, New Jersey: Martindale Hubbell, Inc., 1942), II.

Idaho—(20 Ida. 450; 61 Ida. 9).
Indiana—(117 N. E. 265).
Iowa—
Kansas—Common law marriage is recognized, but the parties are punished for disregarding the statutory requisites of formal marriage (36 Kan. 626).
Michigan—
Mississippi—
Montana—Common law marriage is recognized, and parties marrying without solemnization may make a joint declaration of marriage, which must be acknowledged and recorded, in like manner as a marriage certificate.
Nevada—Common law marriages and those solemnized among people called Friends or Quakers, according to their own forms and practices, are valid.
Ohio—(85 O. 238, 97 N. E. 832).
Oklahoma—(67 Okla. 3); and marriages according to Indian customs are recognized (34 Okla. 807).
Pennsylvania—
South Carolina—(108 S. C. 271).
South Dakota—(37 S. D. 353).
Texas—
Wyoming—Common law marriage would probably be recognized (5 Wyo. 433); though this cannot be stated for certain (16 Wyo. 340); if the common law marriage be contracted elsewhere, and it is valid where contracted, it is valid in Wyoming.

The following states and extra-territorial possessions do not at present recognize common law marriage as valid:

Arkansas—
Arizona—Marriage contracted in Arizona must be under license and solemnized by a person authorized by law, or by someone purporting to act in such capacity and believed in good faith, at least by one of the parties, to be such.
California—Common law marriages consummated prior to 1895 are recognized, but not otherwise; solemnization is necessary for validity at present.
Canal Zone—
Connecticut—Common law marriage would probably not be recognized (93 Conn. 38).
Delaware—Not valid (31 Del. 303, 114 Atl. 215); but if

a non-resident contracted common law marriage elsewhere, and the marriage was valid where contracted, it will be recognized as valid in Delaware.

Hawaii—(27 Fed. [2d] 582).

Illinois—Common law marriage is abolished, but children of such marriages are legitimized by the subsequent legal marriage of their parents.

Kentucky—Common law marriages contracted are not generally recognized, but they are so construed for purposes of recovery and distribution, under special provisions of the Workmen's Act (243 Ky. 694–701, 275 Ky. 559).

Louisiana—(117 La. 967).

Maine—Probably not valid.[34]

Maryland—Not permitted, but if valid where contracted will be recognized as valid in Maryland.

Massachusetts—(127 Mass. 459).

Minnesota—Void since April 26, 1941.

Missouri—Invalid, except when contracted prior to March 31, 1921 (236 S. W. Rep. 1061).

Nebraska—(122 Neb. 805).

New Hampshire—(19 N. H. 257).

New Jersey—Common law marriage may not be contracted after November 30, 1939; but such marriages contracted on or prior to that date are recognized.

New Mexico—

New York—Valid if contracted prior to January 1, 1902; invalid from January 1, 1902 to December 31, 1907, inclusively; valid from January 1, 1908 to April 28, 1933; valid if contracted since April 29, 1933.[35]

North Carolina—(19 N. C. 177).

North Dakota—(23 N. D. 231).

Oregon—

Puerto Rico—

Rhode Island—

Tennessee—

---

[34] As Alford points out, no statute nor court decision has decisively settled this question in Maine, though authors generally concede common law marriage would not be valid in Maine, since the jurisprudence of this State usually conforms to that of the other New England States, none of which recognizes the validity of common law marriage.—*Jus Matrimoniale Comparatum*, n. 398, p. 295, in ff.

[35] Cf. Alford, *loc. cit.*

Utah—
Vermont—(68 Vt. 1).
Virginia—
Washington—
West Virginia—(29 W. Va. 732), but children of such marriages are legitimate (106 W. Va. 615); if contracted in a state where valid, the common law marriage will be recognized as valid in West Virginia (106 W. Va. 615).
Wisconsin—Though the matter has not been passed on by the Supreme Court of the State, the Attorney General has held that common law marriage, or any other form of marriage not in accordance with statutory provisions, is null and void (17 O.A.G. 383).

Since the law of any state may change, it must be remembered that before any ecclesiastical tribunal attempts to decide the validity of a common law marriage, in which the parties are unbaptized, the present law of the state should be consulted.

CHAPTER II

Marriage Under Roman Law and Concubinatus

ARTICLE 1. MARRIAGE AT ROMAN LAW

Marriage at Roman law was defined by Justinian as "*viri et mulieris conjunctio, individuam consuetudinem vitae retinens,*"[1] and by Modestinus as "*conjunctio maris et feminae, et consortium omnis vitae, divini et juris communicatio.*"[2]

For a marriage to be recognized as such at Roman law, it was necessary that it be contracted by Roman citizens, unless a special provision of law allowed otherwise.[3]

For a valid marriage (*justae nuptiae*), the law demanded certain other requisites:[4]

1—Both parties must have reached the age of puberty. Originally this age was determined in each individual case according to the persons involved, but Justinian declared it to be fourteen in males, twelve in females.[5]

2—The parties must conform to the rules of law (*praecepta legum*) concerning impediments.

3—The last, and most important requisite for marriage, was the consent of the parties themselves and of those concerned.[6]

To understand the marriage consent of Roman law it will first

[1] Inst. (1.9) 1.

[2] D. (23.2) 1.

[3] Ulpianus, *Reg.* 5, 3: "Connubium est uxoris iure ducendae facultas;" *Reg.* 5, 4: "Connubium habent cives Romani cum civibus romanis; cum latinis et peregrinis ita, si concessum sit."

[4] Inst. 1.10: "Iustas autem nuptias inter se cives romani contrahunt qui secundum praecepta legum coeunt."

[5] Inst. (1.22) pr; D. (33.1) 24; D. (23.2) 4: "Minorem annis duodecim nuptam tunc legitimam fore cum apud virum explesset duodecim annis."

[6] D. (30.1) 17: "Nuptias non concubitus sed consensus facit." This rule of Ulpian is also reproduced in D. (50.17) de Reg. Juris. Cf. D. (30.2) 2.

be necessary to mention briefly in what marriage consisted under the Roman law. Then, even as now, the betrothal, or engagement to marry, existed as a well-established custom. Then, however, it possessed a legal form, which was not necessary for a valid marriage.[7]

In the time of Justinian, no formal ceremonies were required for entering marriage, except for patricians, senators, and other *illustres.*[8]

The consent of the parties, not otherwise impeded, effected a valid marriage. Matrimonial consent was not looked upon as contractual. And once consent was given, it mattered little whether the ceremonies usually attendant upon marriage were omitted.[9]

Marital cohabitation was an evidence of consent. If cohabitation were begun in view of a promise by the man to marry the woman at a future date, and if, during that cohabitation, children were born of the union, the man was not allowed to eject the woman "without observing the formalities of law." The law further stated that "she shall be his lawful wife and his children also shall be legitimate."[10] The leading of the bride to the house of the groom, *deductio in domum,* was an important ceremony, though necessary only when the marriage had been contracted in the absence of the groom. Thus it was possible for a man to have his proxy give the matrimonial consent in his stead, and conduct the bride to her new home; even though the groom never saw the woman, the marriage was valid.[11]

If the parties were not *sui juris,* the consent of their *patresfamilias* was necessary for the validity of the marriage.[12] Nor did reverential fear of the parent constitute compulsion, as grounds for nullity of the marriage.[13]

---

[7] D. (23.1) 1.

[8] Nov. (74.4) 1; Nov. 117.4.

[9] Cod. (5.4) 2; (5.4) 13; (3.7) 3; (22.5) 4.

[10] Nov. (74.5) pr.

[11] D. (23.2) 5: "Mulierem absenti per litteras ejus vel nuntium posse nubere placet, si in domum ejus deduceretur."

[12] Inst. (1.10) pr; (1.10) 12; D. (23.2) 2.

[13] Cod. (5.4) 14

ARTICLE 2. CONCUBINATUS IN ROMAN LAW

Granting the legal fitness of the parties to marry, the marital consent, *affectio maritalis,* was the efficient cause of a valid marriage. Cohabitation without this *affectio maritalis* was *concubinatus.*[14] This *concubinatus* was the term originally applied to the union of a man and woman who, because of difference of social status, could not enter a valid marriage.[15] Later *concubinatus* was allowed irrespective of the social status of the parties.[16] Though a man might take a woman either as his wife or *concubina,* if the woman were *ingenua,* the union was presumed to be marriage rather than *concubinatus.*[17] By law *concubinatus* was removed from the penal effects of the law punishing adultery,[18] and by law it was restricted to a monogamous union.[19]

Since it was no easy matter to determine true marriage and to distinguish it from concubinage, Cujacius gives the following norms for determining a true marriage:

1—A consideration and comparison of the two parties; for an *ingenuus* is not presumed to have a *libertina* as his wife, but as his *concubina.* Similarly she is presumed a *concubina,* even though *ingenua* " quae corpus suum ante vulgo publicaverit." Similarly she is not presumed a wife, who does not bring to a

---

[14] D. (25.7) 4: "Concubinam ex sola animi destinatione aestimari oportet." D. (32.49) 4: "Parvi autem refert uxori an concubinae quis leget, quae eius causa empta parata sunt: sane enim nisi dignitate nihil interest."

[15] "Quas personas per hanc legem uxores habere non licet concubinas habere jus esto."—*Lex Juliae et Pappiae,* c. 4. This law, enacted in 9 A. D., is quoted in Freisen, *Geschichte des canonischen Eherechts bis zum Verfall der Glossenlitteratur* (2 ed., Padenborn, 1893), p. 47.

[16] D. (25.7) 3: "In concubinatu potest esse et aliena liberta et ingenua et maxime ea quae obscuro loco nata est vel quae quaestum corpore fecit . . ."

[17] D. (25.7) 3: ". . . alioquin si honestae vitae et ingenuam mulierem in concubinatum habere maluerit, sine testatione hoc manifestum faciente non conceditur, sed necesse est si vel uxorem eam habere vel hoc recusantem stuprum cum ea committere."

[18] D. (25.7) 3, 1: "Quia concubinatus per leges nomen assumpsit, extra legis [Juliae de adulteriis] poenam est."

[19] Nov. 18.5, which permits intestate succession to the children born of one concubine; but if there had been more than one, " odio nobis dignus est et talis homo procul ab lege protinus depellendus est."

man's house the "honores et ministeria congruentia dominae," and who is unworthy of his "mensa atque cubili."

2—The reputation and opinion of the neighbors must be considered.

From these norms, it would seem that a great difference of social status would attest to concubinage rather than marriage, if no other determinant proof were available. So too, the reputation which the cohabitation enjoyed in the neighborhood would go a long way in determining whether a specific union were a marriage or concubinage.[20]

ARTICLE 3. THE CHURCH AND CONCUBINATUS

Faced with the problem of *concubinatus* as it existed at Roman law, the Church was forced to legislate in the matter. She did not feel constrained to follow the Roman law of marriage; her doctrine forbade divorce which was recognized at Roman law. Pope Callistus (218–223), a former slave himself, allowed the status of marriage to slaves though Roman law would not.[21] St. Jerome, who died in 420, pointed out the distinction between the law of the Church and Roman law in treating of the divorce of Fabiola: "The laws of the Caesars are very different from the laws of Christ; Papinian bids us do one thing, Paul—our Paul—another." [22]

So it is not unusual that we find the Council of Toledo in 400 A. D., allowing a man to receive Holy Communion, though he had a concubine in his home. This was no relaxation of the Catholic teaching which forbids fornication and adultery. It was merely the taking of a civil institution which the civil law called *concubinatus,* and, seeing therein the requisites for marriage fulfilled, permitting its continuance. "If a man with a faithful wife has a concubine, let him not receive Communion," says the Council; "on the other hand he who has not a wife, and in her place has a

---

[20] Cujacius, *In Lib. XII Resp. Aemilii Papiniani* (Prati, 1837), Comm. ad D. (39.5) 31.

[21] Cf. *infra,* p. 23.

[22] Ep. 77, n. 3—Migne, *Patrologiae Cursus Completus, Series Latina* (221 vols., Parisiis, 1844–1864), XXII, 691. (Henceforth this work will be cited *MPL.*)

concubine, let him not keep away from Communion, provided that he be content to be joined to one woman, either a wife, or a concubine (if he prefer). Let him who lives otherwise be expelled (i.e. from the Church) until he shall cease that practice and return to penance." [23]

Severinus Binus, in commenting on that canon of the Council, says that by the word "concubine" in the text, we are to understand a wife, married without dowry and without external solemnities, but with mutual consent on the part of the man and woman of living together forever. He mentions Old Testament examples of true wives who were called concubines, Agar and Cetura in Genesis XXV, 6. He points out that Justinian in Novel 18, cap. 5, compares concubines to wives who were led in marriage without the solemnity of signing the dowry tablets. Finally referring to St. Augustine's requirements for marriage, he shows that these requirements were really fulfilled in these women whom Roman law called concubines. The requirements of St. Augustine were: First, that each party be unmarried beforehand; second, that there be mutual consent, which will neither be transferable to another, nor preclude the procreation of children; third, that the parties intend to remain thus united until death.[24] Under such conditions it may be easily concluded that the Church considered such unions marriage, though civil law, because of the different social status of the parties, might forbid them under another name.[25]

Following this interpretation of *concubinatus,* a text attributed

[23] "Si quis habens uxorem fidelis concubinam habet, non communicet: ceterum is qui non habet uxorem et pro uxore concubinam habeat, a communione non repellatur, tantum ut unius mulieris aut uxoris aut concubinae, ut ei placuerit, sit conjunctione contentus."—c. 17, Council of Toledo—Mansi, *Sacrorum Conciliorum Nova et Amplissima Collectio* (53 vols. in 59, Parisiis, 1901–1927), III, 1001. (Henceforth this work will be cited Mansi.)

[24] *Notae Severinae Binii ad Conc. Tol.,* c. 17—Mansi III, 1017.

[25] "Porro ipsum Toletanum Concilium multa habet . . . in quarum decima septima quod ponitur de concubina, intellige secundum ea quae Sanctus Augustinus de libro boni conjugali, libro quinto." Such is the commentary of the father of modern Church History, Cardinal Caesar Baronius in his *Annales Ecclesiastici* (37 vols., Vols. I-XXVIII, Barri-Ducis, 1864–1875, Vols. XXIX-XXXVII, Parisiis, 1876–1883).

by Ivo and Gratian to St. Isidore, permits a man to have a concubine.[26] And the legislation of the Council of Toledo is repeated by Halitgar, Archbishop of Cambray, who died in 831,[27] and by the Council of Mainz in 852.[28] The canons issued under the rule of King Edgar in 960, while not stating a general rule, leave it to the individual man to select as his consort one of two women with whom he is living: " Si quis habet uxorem et concubinam, etiam nullus sacerdos ei ullum aliquod officium praestet cum christianis, nisi ad emendationem revertatur; unam sibi retineat, sive uxorem sive concubinam." [29] All of these enactments, it must be stressed, allow concubinage only when the concubine is considered by the Church as a true wife.

Because many did not judge a *concubina* to be a true wife, many Church laws forbid a man to live with one. St. Leo, who died in 458, declared that " a concubine is not the same as a wife." [30] St. Nicephorous (806–815), Patriarch of Constantinople, declares the Church should have nothing to do with a man who refuses to marry his *concubina* with the Sacramental rite.[31] The various enactments of Councils which forbid marriages without the presence of a priest would also indirectly militate against the union of a man with a *concubina*.[32]

[26] " Christiano non dicam plurimas, sed nec duas simul habere licitum est, nisi unam tantum aut uxorem, aut certe, loco uxoris, si conjunx deest, concubinam."—*Decretum Ivonis*, l. VIII, c. 66—*MPL*, CLXI, 598; c. 5, D. XXXIV.

[27] *De Poenitentia* l. IV, c. 12—*MPL*, CV, 683.

[28] Council of Mainz, c. 15—*Monumenta Germaniae Historica, Leges* (ed. Societas Aperiendis Fontibus Rerum Germanicarum Medii Aevi, 5 vols., Lipsiae, 1925), I, 415. (Henceforth this work will be cited *MGH, Leges*.)

[29] *Canones editi sub R. Edgaro*, c. 19, *De Poenitentia*—Wilkins, *Concilia Magnae Brittaniae et Hiberniae* (4 vols., London, 1737), I, 232. (Henceforth this work will be cited Wilkins.)

[30] *Ep. 167* (ad Rusticum) *MPL*, LIV, 124; Jaffé, *Regesta Pontificum Romanorum* (ed. secundam correctam et auctam auspiciis Gulielmi Wattenbach curaverunt Kaltenbrunner [ad annum 590], Ewald [anno 590–882], Lowenfeld [882–1198], Lipsiae, 1881), JK, n. 554. (Henceforth JK, JE, JL will signify the authors of this work.)

[31] *Ex constitutionibus eiusdem* (Nicephori) *et sanctorum cum eo patrum*, c. 90—Pitra, *Iuris Ecclesiastice Graecorum Historia et Monumenta* (2 vols., Romae, 1864–1868), II, 336.

[32] Cf. *infra*, pp. 31–32.

Only under those conditions and in those circumstances did the Church allow *concubinatus* when it was apparent that the union was in reality a marriage, though denied the name of marriage by civil law. Whenever *concubinatus* was taken in the sense of modern concubinage, namely, a non-permanent extramarital relationship, the Church vehemently condemned and forbade it.[33]

[33] "Grave peccatum est, omnes solutos concubinas habere; gravissimum vero, et in hujus magni Sacramenti singularem contemptum admissum, uxoratos quoque in hoc damnationis statu vivere, accaudere eas quandoque domi etiam cum uxoribus alere et retinere."—Conc. Trident., sess. XXIV, *de ref. matrim.,* c. 8. Cf. Insodowski, "Quid Momenti Habuerit Christianismus Ad Ius Romanum Matrimoniale Evolvendum"—*Acta Congressus Iuridici Internationalis* (5 vols., Romae: Apud Custodiam Librariam Pont. Instituti Utriusque Iuris, 1935–1937), II, 52–54.

CHAPTER III

Legislation Up to the Council of Trent

ARTICLE 1. PRIOR TO THE TIME OF GRATIAN

Common law marriage, because devoid of formal ceremonies, in canonical terminology is called a clandestine marriage. Though the term clandestine marriage has been used to connote other types of marriage, e.g., those contracted in *facie ecclesiae* but without the publication of the banns, the term will be used in this treatise to signify a marriage performed without the intervention of the Church authorities, a marriage without the formal ceremonial requisites demanded by ecclesiastical authority. It was in this sense used by the Council of Trent and accepted by canonical authors.[1]

Over this type of marriage as over all formal types, among Christians, Christ gave to His Church the exclusive power of legislation and adjudication, and with all the respect, caution and vigilance due to marriage, the Church has wielded this power.[2]

The natural law demands for marriage only that the parties be competent to marry, that they express consent reciprocally, and that this consent be manifested through words, signs or any equivalent way.[3] Yet the social aspects of the marital status de-

[1] Cf. c. 3, X, *de clandestina desponsatione,* IV, 3; Conc. Trident., sess. XXIV, *de ref. matrim.*, c. 1; Gasparri, *Tractatus Canonicus de Matrimonio,* ed. nova ad mentem Codicis I. C. (2 vols., Romae [Civitate Vaticana]: Typis Polyglottis Vaticanis, 1932), I, n. 49.

[2] "Christus igitur, cum ad talem ac tantam excellentiam matrimonia renovavisset, totam ipsorum disciplinam Ecclesiae credidit et commendavit. Quae potestatem in conjugia Christianorum omni cum tempore, tum loco exercuit, atque ita exercuit, ut illam propriam eius esse appareret, nec hominum concessu quaesitum, sed auctoris sui voluntate divinitus adeptam." —Leo XIII, ep. encycl. *Arcanum Divinae,* 10 feb. 1880—*Fontes,* n. 580.

[3] DeSmet, *De Sponsalibus et Matrimonio,* ed. quarta inde a codice altera (Brugis: Car. Beyaert, Editor Pontificius, 1927), n. 103.

mand, in an organized society, that competent social authority safeguard against abuses of the exercise of the natural right to marry. Thus Christ gave the discipline of Christian marriage over to His Church. The Church, appreciating full well the evils of clandestine marriage, always abhorred and prohibited them, though until the sixteenth century, she did not demand the form of marriage now common in the Catholic Church.[4]

During the persecutions which prevailed during the first few centuries of the Church's existence, neither the need nor the opportunity to exercise widespread jurisdiction presented itself. Yet, even in the infant Church, reference was made to the Christian celebratoin of marriage by St. Ignatius, Bishop of Antioch, who died in 107.[5] In the following century Tertullian (died 223–240? A. D.), considered Christian marriage as a public religious act subject to ecclesiastical control,[6] and in his *De Pudicitia*,[7] he contrasts the pagan custom of marriage with the Christian custom, mentioning the latter as a marriage "*apud ecclesiam professae.*"

The Christian teaching that the marital union of a Christian man and woman signified the union between Christ and His Church had been explained by Saint Paul,[8] and had instilled in the minds of the early Christians the reverence due the marriage union. The presence of a minister of Christ was demanded at the formation of the union, a union which was more than the

[4] "Tametsi dubitandum non est clandestina matrimonia libero contrahentium consensu facta, rata et vera esse matrimonia quamdiu ecclesia ea irrita non fecit, nihilominus Ecclesia ex iustissimis causis illa semper detestata est atque prohibita . . ."—Conc. Trident., sess. XXIV. *de ref. matrim.*, c. 1.

[5] "Decet vero ut sponsi et sponsae de sententia episcopi conjugium faciant ut matrimonium fit secundum Dominum non secundum concupiscentiam."—*Ep. ad Polycarpum*, V—Migne, *Patrologiae Cursus Completus, Series Graeca* (162 vols., Parisiis, 1856–1866), V, 963. (Henceforth this work will be cited *MPG.*)

[6] "Unde sufficiamus ad enarrandum felicitatem eius matrimonii, quod Ecclesia consiliat, et confirmat oblatio, et obsignat benedictio, angeli renuntiant, Pater vero rato habet."—*Ad Uxorem*, lib. II, c. 9—*MPL*, I, 1302.

[7] C. 4—*MPL* II, 987. This work was written while Tertullian was a heretic (217–222).

[8] Eph. V, 22–31.

legal contract of pagan rite, for it was a union by which a new family was formed as a new cell in the Mystical Body of Christ.[9]

For the same reason the Church did not feel constrained to follow the civil laws which forbid persons of different social status to marry. For in the eyes of the Church all men through Baptism become equally sons of God, therefore equally brothers despite varied social status. So it was that Pope St. Callistus (218–223), a former slave himself, was reproached for having allowed women of high social standing to marry freedmen or slaves.[10] The reproach proved the fact that the Pontiff had adjudged such people free to intermarry. Because such marriages, adverse to the rulings of civil law, were necessarily secret, a proof of the Church's tolerance of civilly clandestine marriages is also afforded in the same instance.

Following the teaching of the Fathers concerning the sacredness of marriage, the Popes throughout the ages issued prominent pronouncements against secret and clandestine marriages. Pope Eutichianus (275–283),[11] Pope St. Siricius (384–398),[12] Pope St. Leo the Great (440–461),[13] and Pope Hormisdas (514–523),[14] all inveigh against clandestine marriages.

As mentioned in the preceding chapter, Roman law recognized clandestine marriages. From the fifth century on, the Church encountered Teutonic law as civil legislation for some of her subjects. According to this law, marriage was usually accompanied by the transfer of guardianship (*mundium*) of the bride from her parents or legal custodians to the groom. This transfer

[9] Ballini, *Il Valore Giuridico Della Celebrazione Nuziale Cristiana Dal Primo Secolo All'eta Giustinianea*, Pubblicazioni Dell' Universita Cattolica Del S. Cuore: Serie Seconda: Scienze Giuridica, Vol. LXIV (Milano: Societa Editrice—Vita e Pensiero, 1937), 11, 12.

[10] Hippolytus, *Philosophumena*, lib. IX, c. 12—*MPG*, XVI, 3386.

[11] *Exhortatio ad Presbyteros:* "Nullus vestrum ad nuptias eat: omnibus denuntiate ut nullus nisi publice celebratis nuptiis uxorem ducat."—*MPL* V, 1167; JK, n. 156.

[12] *Ep. I ad Himer*, c. 4—JK, n. 255; *MPL*, XIII, 1136; Mansi, III, 657.

[13] Inq. IV, *Ep. 167* (ad Rusticum)—JK, n. 544; *MPL*, LIV, 1204; Mansi, VI, 402.

[14] "Nullus fidelis cuiuscumque conditione sit, occulte nuptias faciat, sed benedictione accepta a sacerdote, publice nubat in Domino."—JK, n. 868; Mansi VIII, 530.

of *mundium* which was similar to the *manus* of Roman law, required the observance of certain prescribed formalities. Without these formalities the marriage would not be a legal one (*matrimonium legitimum*). In the Lombard law, which prevailed in Italy from 568 until 774, and in Lombardy much longer, the Fürsprecher, or *orator* (similar to our notary), questioned the parties to the marriage concerning their intention of entering marriage.[15] Yet even though this *mundium* was not transferred, the marriage was valid.[16] Whenever the woman was not transferred by her legal guardian (*mundoaldus*), the establishment of conjugal life was necessary. For the *traditio* of the woman was required, either by the transfer of the *mundium,* or by the actual establishment of conjugal life (*ambulavit ad maritum*). Mere consent was not enough.[17]

Despite what civil law might demand, the Church declared that consent and consent alone constituted a valid marriage, that neither consummation nor formal ceremonies were necessary. Not merely a question of legislative policy, this doctrine had dogmatic implications, for should consummation be required for a valid marriage, the union of the Blessed Virgin Mary and Saint Joseph would not have been a true marriage.[18] But the Church has always held that theirs was a true marriage. St. Ambrose, who died in 397 A. D., speaking of this marriage, stated that the nuptial agreement alone constituted a real marital contract.[19] And St. Augustine, Bishop of Hippo from 396 until 430, taught that the lack of carnal relations did not dissolve the bond of marriage.[20] The principle clearly stated, "*Matrimonium non*

[15] Cartularium Langobardorum, Formula 16—*MGH, Leges,* IV, 599.

[16] Lex Baiuwariorum, VIII, 17—*MGH, Leges,* III, 301; *Lex Frisonum,* IX, 11—*ibid.,* p. 665; *Lex Thuringorum,* 47—*ibid.,* V, 135.

[17] Joyce, *Christian Marriage,* 48–52.

[18] Luke, II: 5.

[19] *De Institutione Virginis,* lib. I, c. VI, 41–42—*MPL,* XVI, 316. St. Ambrose also advocated that Christian marriage should be "sanctified by the priestly veil and benediction."—*Ep. ad Vigil.,* c. VII—*MPL,* XVI, 985.

[20] *De Nuptiis et Concupiscentia,* lib. I, c. 11—*MPL,* XLIV, 224; *Corpus Scriptorum Ecclesiasticorum Latinorum* (68 vols., Vindebonae, 1866–1936), XLII, 224. (Henceforth this work will be cited *CSEL.*) St. Augustine also recommends that the bishop sign the nuptial tablets which were drawn up when two parties married—*Sermo* 332, n. 4—*MPL,* XXXVIII, 1463.

facit coitus sed voluntas," was taught in the same century by an unknown author in a work which has been falsely attributed to St. John Chrysostom.[21] In a like vein, St. Isidore, Bishop of Seville, who died in 636 A. D., defines married persons ". . . in view of the initial plighting of their troth, even though consummation has not taken place." [22]

At length in 866, Pope Nicholas I issued what since has become a famous letter, in replying to certain questions sent to him by the Christians in Bulgaria. Certain Greek priests had assured the people that no marriage was valid unless it had been blessed by a priest. The Pope in replying, said that the essential factor in marriage was the consent and if consent were lacking no ceremonies could effect a marriage. " Let the simple consent of those whose wedding is in question be sufficient, as the (*civil*) laws prescribe," said the Pope,[23] thus indicating the sufficiency of consent for the formation of the marital contract, and at the same time indicating the practice of the Church to conform to civil law, when the civil law accorded with the Church's teaching.

This compliance with civil regulations is also evidenced in a letter of Bishop Atto of Vercelli, about 950 A. D., to a fellow bishop.[24] Though, as we have pointed out in reference to Roman and Germanic laws, the Church did not feel bound to follow the regulations of civil authority as regards marriage, yet it was not uncommon that some ecclesiastical authorities should counsel that civil laws be complied with in practice. Perhaps it was to avoid unnecessary trouble. Besides the insinuation of Pope St. Nicho-

---

[21] *Opus Imperfectum in Mattheum,* Hom. XXXII, cap. XIX—*MPG,* LVI, 802.

[22] *Etymologiarum,* lib. IX, cap. VII, 9—*MPL,* LXXXII, 365.

[23] ". . . ac per hoc sufficiat secundum leges solus eorum consensus, de quorum conjunctionibus agatur. Qui consensus si solus in nuptiis forte defuerit, cetera omnia etiam cum ipso coitu celebrata frustrantur . . ."—*Responsa ad Consulta Bulgorum,* cap. 3—JE 2812; Mansi V, 403; c. 27, q. 2; *MPL,* CXIX, 980; Denziger-Bannwart-Umberg, *Enchiridion Symbolorum* (ed. 18–20, Friburgi Brisgoviae: Herder & Co., 1932), p. 162, n. 334. (Henceforth this work will be cited Denziger.)

[24] *Ep. ad Azonem* (V): "Matrimonium enim est conjugium justa conventio et condicio: eos vero qui nefario et exsecrabili coitu contra leges et mores permiscentur omnino separari oportet, quoniam nec vir nec uxor poterit esse in huiusmodi."—*MPL,* CXXXIV, 109.

las and the advice of Bishop Atto, we find Ivo of Chartres (who died in 1116) quoting the words of Pope John VIII (872–882), to the Emperor Louis II: "What is done in defiance of the law may be set aside by the law." [25] This declaration of nullity of a marriage formed against the prescriptions of civil law contradicts the teaching of Tertullian, Callistus and others, thus indicating that the legislation of the Church and its relation to civil law had not yet reached an organic stabilization and complete state of independence.[26]

ARTICLE 2. THE COPULA THEORY

About the same time that the above-mentioned question was troubling the Church, another more involved problem arose. The Church had taught that consent effected a marriage, even though consummation had not taken place. From the ninth century on, there arose a dispute as to the necessity of consummation of marriage, if not to constitute a valid marriage, at least to perfect a union which through consent was but inchoate. The theory requiring copula for the validity of marriage was called the copula theory (*copulatheoria*). Its importance is apparent, for if true, this theory would invalidate an unconsummated union, or at least it would declare such a marriage an imperfect one and, therefore, not a diriment impediment to another marital union.

An eminent Frankish prelate, Hincmar of Rheims (who died in 862), in his treatise *De Nuptiis Stephani et Filiae Regimundi Regis,* first proposed the theory. Stephen had previously entered a clandestine marriage with another woman, whose identity he refused to disclose. Feeling in conscience bound to this first woman, he refused to consummate the second union with the daughter of King Regimund. His refusal to disclose the name of his partner in the first union prevented legal proof of the existence of a marriage bond, and the validity of the second marriage remained in doubt. Hincmar's work was an answer to an appeal made by the Council of Touzy, in 860. He maintained the second marriage was not a real marriage but merely an inceptive one,

---

[25] "Quod contra leges presumitur, per leges dissolvi meretur"—Ivo, *Decretum* IV, 179, and *Panormia,* II, 150; c. 10, D. X; JE 3011.

[26] Joyce, *Christian Marriage,* 53.

since without consummation he allowed only an inceptive, not a real marriage.[27]

In Chapters 1 to 50 of Causa XXVII, Gratian devotes himself at length to the question. He advances the arguments on either side of the question concerning the necessity of consummation for a real marriage. His conclusion follows the theory of Hincmar, and he states that with two exceptions (which will be mentioned later), marriage is effected not by consent, but by carnal consummation.[28]

Gratian, as had Hincmar before him, appeals to the authority of St. Augustine, but St. Augustine's writings, as we now know them, do not justify such an appeal,[29] and to St. Leo, though he quotes the Pope in a sense directly opposite to the authentic text,[30] to support the conclusion he draws. In Chapters 19–21 of the same passage, viz. C. XXVII, q. 2, Gratian cites different instances in which the dissolution of a non-consummated marriage is possible, concluding from these cases that marriage effected by consent alone is not a perfect marriage.[31] To such a marriage,

---

[27] *De Nuptiis Stephani et Filiae Regimundi Regis:* "Nec habeant in se Christi et Ecclesiae sacramentum, sicut beatus Augustinus dicit, si se nuptialiter non utuntur, id est, si eas non subsequitur commixtio sexuum."—*MPL,* CXXVI, 137; *MGH, Epistolae* (ed. Societas Aperiendis Fontibus Rerum Germanicarum Medii Aevi, 8 vols., Vol. VIII [*Karolini Aevi,* VI], Berolini: Weidmanns, 1939), 93.

[28] For a full treatment of the question, cf. DeSmet, *De Sponsalibus et Matrimonio,* nn. 96–99; Joyce, *Christian Marriage,* 56–61.

[29] "Non est dubium illam mulierem non pertinere ad matrimonium, cum qua non fuisse commixtio sexus."—c. 16, C. XXVII, q. 2. This saying Gratian attributes to St. Augustine, though it is not found in any of his writings. Cf. Joyce, *op. cit.,* 56.

[30] The text of St. Leo, *Ep. 167* (ad Rusticum): "Unde cum societas nuptiarum ita ab initio constituta sit, ut praeter sexum conjunctionem haberet in se Christi et Ecclesiae sacramentum, dubium non est eam mulierem non pertinere ad matrimonium, in qua docetur nuptiale non fuisse mysterium"—*MPL,* LIV, 1204; JK, 544.

Gratian inserts a ***non*** which completely alters the sense and significance of the passage: "Unde cum ab initio societas nuptiarum ita ab initio constituta sit, ut praeter sexum conjunctionem ***non*** habeant in se nuptiae conjunctionis Christi et Ecclesiae sacramentum . . . etc."—c. 17, C. XXVII, 2.

[31] *Dictum* p. c. 24, C. XVII, q. 2.

formed by consent alone, Gratian would give only the force of an inceptive marriage. "It must be known," he says, "that marriage commences with mutual consent, and is made perfect by carnal intercourse; whence it follows that the contract produces marriage, indeed, but only an inceptive one, while the conjugal act brings into being marriage that is ratified." [32] The Pseudo-Chrysostom adage, "Matrimonium non facit coitus sed voluntas," Gratian interprets to mean that coition without consent or agreement to marry does not constitute a marriage, and that the antecedent intention to marry, and the preliminary conjugal contract gave reason to say that at the moment of coition a woman is married to her husband, or contracts marriage.[33]

With this theory of the necessity of the consummation for the perfection of marriage, it might be supposed that Gratian would allow every couple, who had married only by consent, to separate and go their respective ways to other unions. But Gratian, in the remaining chapters of this portion of his work, excepts two cases, in which he holds that the woman cannot retract or dissolve the marriage with her first husband, namely, in the case wherein a woman was abducted from her first husband, in which case she must be restored to him; and secondly, when the first husband has already taken her into his home and they have received the veil and blessing together, they cannot separate, for as he says, "the rupture in that case would violate the blessing that the priest gave to the bride." [34]

Except for these two cases, Gratian's teaching maintains that an unconsummated clandestine marriage would not be binding as would a consummated, or perfect marriage; and the parties to

---

[32] "Sciendum est, quod conjugium desponsatione initiatur, commixtione perficitur; under inter sponsum et sponsam conjugium est, sed initiatum; inter copulatos est conjugium ratum "—*Dictum* ad c. 34, XXVII, q. 2.

[33] "Coitus sine voluntate contrahendi matrimonium et defloratio virginis sine pactione conjugali non facit matrimonium, sed praecedens voluntas contrahendi matrimonium et conjugalis pactio facit ut mulier in defloratione suae virginitatis vel in coitu dicatur nubere viro, vel nuptias celebrare"—*Dictum* p. c. 45, C. XXVII, q. 2.

[34] *Dictum* p. c. 50, C. XXVII, q. 2. However, even in these cases, Gratian maintains that the parties are not united in a true and complete marriage.

the imperfect, or inceptive unions, could marry someone else, should they so choose.[35]

Ivo of Chartres (who died in 1116) had rejected the theory requiring copula,[36] as had also St. Peter Damian (who died in 1072),[37] citing traditional passages from St. Ambrose and St. Isidore. Following these men, Peter the Lombard championed the cause against the copula theory. In his *Book of the Sentences,* he developed the distinction between betrothal and marriage, that is between *verba de praesenti* and *verba de futuro,* and maintained that *verba de futuro* did not constitute marriage. At the same time he insisted that consent expressed through words of present tense did effect a marriage contract, independently of any physical consummation.[38]

This dispute between Gratian and the canonists of the School of Bologna, on the one hand,[39] and Peter the Lombard and the School of Paris on the other,[40] was decided by Pope Alexander III (1159–1181), in a letter to the Archbishop of Salerno. Prior to his election the Pope had been Roland Bandinelli, Magister at the School of Bologna, and therefore inclinded towards the view

[35] In comparatively recent times, the theory of Gratian was upheld by Freisen, though in a later edition of his work, he retracts his opinion as being against the traditional doctrine of the Church. Freisen, *Geschichte des canonischen Eherects bis zum Verfall der Glossenlitteratur* (2 ed., Paderborn, 1893), Preface, pp. XXIII–XXVI.

[36] *Ep.* 246—*MPL,* CLXII, 253.

[37] Opusc. 41: *De Tempore Celebrandi Nuptias—MPL,* CXLV, 660.

[38] IV *Sent. d.* XXVII: "Efficiens causa matrimonii est consensus, non quilibet, sed per verba expressus, nec de futuro, sed de praesenti. Si enim consentiunt in futurum dicentes: Accipiam te in virum: et Ego te in uxorem: non est iste consensus efficax matrimonii . . . Quidam tamen asserunt verum conjugium non contrahi ante traductionem et carnalem copulam . . . His autem respondeo: Fit aliquando desponsatio, ubi est compromissio viri et mulieris de contrahendo matrimonio: non est autem ibi consensus de praesenti. Est et desponsatio habens consensum de praesenti, id est pactionem conjugalem, quae sola facit conjugium."—*MPL,* CXCII, 9; *Petri Lombardi Libri IV Sententiarum* (2 ed., 2 vols., ad Claras Aquas ex typographis collegii S. Bonaventurae, 1916), II, 917, 918, 921.

[39] For other Bolognese authors, cf. Freisen, *Geschichte des canonischen Eherects,* pp. XXVIII–XXXIV.

[40] Cf. DeSmet, *De Sponsalibus et Matrimonio,* n. 98.

demanding copula for the perfection of marriage.[41] When elevated to the Papacy, however, he adopted an intermediate theory, granting on the one hand the nature of a real marriage and of a sacrament to an unconsummated union, and on the other, refusing absolute indissolubility to an unconsummated marriage. Thus, when the Archbishop of Salerno asked if a woman might marry another man, when to one she had already given a marital consent *per verba de praesenti,* without the sanction of an oath attached to the promise, and without the union having been consummated, the Pontiff replied: "If a lawful consent *de praesenti* has been exchanged between a man and a woman (with the formalities which are commonly observed, viz., in the presence of a priest, or even a notary, as is also the custom in certain parts) . . . it is not lawful for the woman to marry another. And if she should have married another man, even though this union be consummated, she must be separated from him, and compelled by the threat of ecclesiastical censures to return to the first, even though the contrary opinion is maintained in some quarters, and some judgments to the contrary have been given by our predecessors." [42]

In another decision, Pope Alexander III decreed that if a man and woman promise that from henceforth they will have each other as man and wife, the contract is one of matrimony *de praesenti.*[43]

Pope Innocent III (1198–1216) likewise held, in 1198, that marriage was lawfully contracted by words of present tense.[44]

---

[41] *Ibid.*

[42] "Consultationi tuae taliter respondemus, quod si inter virum et mulierem legitimus consensus (sub ea solemnitate quae fieri solet, praesente scilicet sacerdote aut etiam notario, sicut etiam in quibusdam locis adhuc observetur, coram idoneis testibus) interveniat . . . sive sit iuramentum interpositum sive non, non licet mulieri alii nubere. Et si nupserit, etiam si carnalis copula sit secuta, ab eo separari debet, et, ut ad primum redeat, ecclesiastica districtione compelli, quamvis (alii) aliter (sentiant et, aliter etiam) a quibusdam praedecessoribus nostris sit aliquando indicatum."—c. 3, X, *de sponsa duorum,* IV, 4: JL 14091. The words in parentheses in this quotation were not included by St. Raymond of Pennafort, when he included the letter in the Gregorian Decretals; cf. Friedberg edition.

[43] c. 9, X, *de sponsa duorum,* IV, 4: JL 13872.

[44] *Ep. Brixiensi*—c. 25, X, *de sponsalibus et matrimonio,* IV, 1; Potthast, *Regesta Pontificum* (2 vols., Berolini, 1874), n. 24. (Henceforth this work will be cited Potthast.)

And Pope Honorius III (1216–1227) declared a marriage contracted by words of present tense was not dissolved by a subsequent marriage which was consummated, even though the first union was unconsummated.[45]

Thus the problem of the constitutive element of marriage, one of the knottiest in the history of matrimonial legislation, was settled once and for all. Since it has been determined that consent alone effects a valid marriage, it is apparent that any common law marriage would not fail in the eyes of the Church merely on the grounds of non-consummation; by the same token cohabitation would not be required if it could be proven that consent *de praesenti* had actually transpired between the two parties.

ARTICLE 3. FROM THE 13TH CENTURY TO THE COUNCIL OF TRENT

The foregoing problem only accentuated the legislation of the Church against clandestine marriages, since it was apparent that the evils consequent upon such unions were growing apace with the extension of the Church. Unless a clandestine marriage were admitted by both parties, or celebrated in such a manner that it might be proven by witnesses, either of the parties might successfully repudiate such a contract.[46]

As the centuries passed the legislation became more frequent. Contemporary with Pope Nicholas I,[47] the Pseudo-Isidorian authors had counselled that marriage be contracted in public, with the blessing of the priest and "*consilio multorum bonorum hominum.*" [48] This priestly blessing had also been advised by the Council of London in 944 A. D.[49] In 1076, the Council of Winchester, while not declaring clandestine marriages null, had said

---

[45] *Ep. Cenomanensi*—c. 31, X, *de sponsalibus et matrimonio,* IV, 1; Potthast, 9662.

[46] c. 1, X, *de clandestina desponsatione,* IV, 3, citing the Council of Arles (*Arletensi* or *Agathensi?*), stated that the presumption did not favor a clandestine marriage, the burden of proof resting on the party who claimed such a union had been contracted.

[47] Cf. *supra,* p. 25.

[48] *Capitularium Collectio Benedictus Levitae,* l. III, c. 179—*MPL,* XCVII, 820; *MGH, Leges,* II, pars altera, 113.

[49] Wilkins, I, 217.

that in the external forum they would be treated as such; it may be presumed that proof to the contrary would be admitted.[50]

Forty years later, in November, 1215, in an endeavor to eradicate the evils of clandestine marriages, the Fourth Lateran Council decreed that banns should be published publicly in Church by a priest, and that time should be allowed for the revelation of any known impediments to the contemplated marriage. Those who contracted marriage against the provisions of this Council were to be punished as the circumstances demanded.[51]

As had this general Council, so too, numerous local councils and synods strove to check by legislative and punitive measures the ever growing evil. Throughout the Continent and the English Isles, bishops in local and provincial synods forbade secret marriages.[52]

Following the lead of the Lateran Council, many local councils prescribed the publication of the banns prior to the celebration of the marriage.[53] Lest the enactments be taken too lightly, penal

---

[50] Hardouin, *Acta Conciliorum et Epistolae Decretales ac Constitutiones Summorum Pontificium* (12 vols., Parisiis, 1715), VIa, 1562. (Henceforth this work will be cited Hardouin.)

[51] c. 51, IV. Conc. Lateran.—Mansi, XX, 1038, 1039; c. 3, X, *de clandestina desponsatione,* IV, 3.

[52] *In England:* Council of London (944)—Wilkins, I, 217; Council of London (1200)—*ibid.,* 507; Council of Durham (1220)—*ibid.,* 581; Council of Oxford (1222)—*ibid.,* 595; Thomas, Archbishop of Canterbury, *Monitio per edictum publicum* (1455)—Mansi, XXXII, 161.

In France: Council of Langeais (1278), c. 3—Mansi, XXIV, 212; Council of Bourges (1286), c. 2—*ibid.,* 627; Council of Narbonne (1374), c. 22—*ibid.,* XXXVI, 605.

In Germany: Council of Salzburg (1291)—Mansi, XXIV, 1075; Council of Salzburg (1420)—*ibid.,* 1013; in this first mentioned Council of Salzburg, Archbishop Conrad had required six witnesses for marriages and required that notice of a marriage which had been performed be given to the parish priest within one month after the performance of the marriage; the latter Council of Salzburg required the presence of the priest at the marriage.

[53] Provincial Council of Scotland (1225), c. 82—Wilkins, I, 618; Synod of *Sodorenses* (1291), c. 27—Wilkins, II, 178; Synodal Constitutions of Henry Woodloke, Bishop of Winton (1308)—*ibid.,* 295; Provincial Council of Canterbury (1328)—*ibid.,* 554; Provincial Council of Treves (1368)—

sanctions were often attached to the synodal laws. Some of these were directed against the priest who might assist at clandestine unions, the usual penalty being suspension from the sacerdotal duties for a three-year period.[54] Nor did the parties themselves escape the legislative wrath against secret marriages. Nearly all of the councils punished them, sometimes with indeterminate penalties, though usually with excommunication.[55] Thus the Council of Exeter, held in 1287, after prohibiting both betrothals and marriages which are not solemnly contracted, describes the evils consequent upon such unions together with the punishment the bishop thought fit to declare: ". . . nonnulla animarum pericula contigit pluries evenire, cum non appareant legitimi testes, per quos contractus posset probari; multoties evenit, ut conjuncti legitimi separentur, et illegitimi conjuncti; cum suarum tolerentur pericula animarum, eo quod ecclesiasticus judex nequit in dubiis certam ferre sententiam: omnes talia matrimonia contrahentes ab ingressu ecclesiae (suspendimus) salva nihilominus poena concilii generalis soboli impositis ex talibus nuptiis procreatae." [56]

The leaders of the Church soon realized that all such measures, short of declaring the nullity of clandestine marriages, were in vain. When the Protestant defection from the Church occurred, the leaders of the heresies and schisms chose as one point of

---

Mansi, XXIII, 29; Provincial Council of Magdeburg (1370)—Mansi, XXVI, 583. This last mentioned Council demanded that the banns be announced by the proper priests (*proprii sacerdotes*) of the parties to the marriage.

[54] Council of London (1175)—Bail, *Summa Conciliorum Omnium* (2 vols., Patavii, 1723), II, 411, 2, d; Council of Canterbury (1328)—Wilkins, II, 554.

[55] Provincial Council of Treves (1227)—Mansi, XXIII, 29; General Council of London (1268), c. 13—Wilkins, II, 8; Council of Bourges (1286)—Mansi, XXIV, 64; Council of Exeter (1287)—Wilkins, II, 136; Council of Salzburg (1291), c. 1—Mansi, XXIV, 1075; Council of London (1342)—Wilkins, II, 707; Council of Prague (1355)—Mansi, XXVI, 401; Constitutions of John Thornsby, Archbishop of York (1367)—Wilkins, III, 71; Council of Magdeburg (1370), c. 32—Mansi, XXVI, 583; Council of Narbonne (1374)—Mansi, XXVI, 605.

[56] Wilkins, II, 125.

attack the Catholic legislation permitting the validity of clandestine marriages.[57]

[57] It must be admitted, however, that the stress laid upon clandestinity of marriage by the Protestants was directed towards those marriages contracted without parental consent, since for them this lack of parental consent constituted clandestinity; cf. Joyce, *op. cit.*, pp. 115–119.

CHAPTER IV

Legislation from the Council of Trent to the Code

ARTICLE 1. FROM THE DECREE TAMETSI, TO THE DECREE NE TEMERE

On January 4, 1564, the Council of Trent reassembled after a long interruption. The legislation concerning clandestine marriages was one of the major problems with which the assembled prelates had to cope. The first proposed draft for laws against such unions declared that all marriages in the future which were contracted without three witnesses should be invalid and null.[1]

During a heated debate which lasted for three months, the original draft was altered three times. Four drafts in all were considered before the Fathers of the Council finally agreed; even in reaching a final decision in favor of a decree against the validity of clandestine marriages, the opposition was still strong.[2]

The twenty-fourth session of the Council, on November 11, 1563, finally adopted a decree which was approved by the reigning Pope Pius IV, in a Bull "*Benedictus Deus*," which confirmed the decrees of the Council.[3]

This decree, known from its opening word as the *Tametsi*, stated: "Although it is not to be doubted that clandestine mar-

---

[1] "Sacrosancta Dei Ecclesia statuit et decernit ea matrimonia quae in posterum clam non adhibitis testibus contrahuntur irrita fore et nulla . . ." —*Concilii Tridentini Diariorum, Actorum, Epistolarum Tracta'uum Nova Collectio* (ed. Societas Gorresiana, 13 vols., Friburgi Brisgoviae: B. Herder, 1901–1938), IX, 939.

[2] For a complete history of the debate in the Council, cf. *Conc. Trident. Diariorum . . . Nova Collectio*, IX, 640–1152; also Carberry, *The Juridical Form of Marriage*, The Catholic University of America Canon Law Studies, n. 84 (Washington: The Catholic Univ. of America, 1934), pp. 20–23.

[3] *Canones et Decreta Sacrosancti Oecumenici Concilii Tridentini sub Paulo III, Iulio III, et Pio IV Pontificibus Maximis*, editio Stereotypa (Ratisbonae, 1903), 205.

riages made with the free consent of the contracting parties are valid and true marriages so long as the Church has not rendered them invalid; and consequently, that those persons are justly to be condemned, as the Holy Synod doth condemn them with anathema, who deny that such marriages are true and valid; . . . nevertheless, the holy church of God has for reasons most just, at all times detested and prohibited such marriages; . . . those who shall attempt to contract marriage otherwise than in the presence of the parish priest, or of some other priest by permission of the said parish priest or of the Ordinary, and in the presence of two or three witnesses; the Holy Synod renders such wholly incapable of such contracting and declares such contracts invalid and null, as by the present decree It invalidates and annuls them."[4]

By this decree clandestine marriages of Christians in the future would be rendered invalid by virtue of the inhabilitation of the parties stated by the Council. Yet the decree did not immediately affect the entire world, for it had been decided by the Council that the law was binding only in those parishes where it was promulgated. The Ordinary was to see to it that the decree was published in each parish; thirty days after such promulgation, the decree was to have the force of law.[5]

Though it had been expected that the decree would be published throughout the world, such was not the case. Several countries never published it, some published it within certain districts, but not in others.[6] Instead of the desired remedy against clandestine marriages, a confused situation arose, since such marriages were still valid in these regions wherein the *Tametsi* had not been published.[7] In those regions where the *Tametsi* was

---

[4] Conc. Trident., sess. XXIV, *de ref. matrim.*, c. 1—*Canones et Decreta Sacrosancti Oecumenici Concilii Tridentini*, 137; Waterworth, *The Canons and Decrees of the Sacred and Oecumenical Council of Trent* (New York and London, 1848), 196, 197.

[5] Conc. Trident., sess. XXIX, *de ref. matrim.*, c. 1.

[6] For an enumeration of the places wherein the *Tametsi* was published, cf. Wernz, *Jus Decretalium*, vol. IV, *Ius Matrimoniale Eccles. Catholicae* (Romae, 1904), 237–244.

[7] S. C. Concilii, 18 ian. 1663 (*Ad Ep. Tricarien.*)—*Collectanea S. Congregationis de Propaganda Fide* (2 vols., Romae, 1907), n. 149. (Hence-

published, any clandestine union of two Catholics (that is, lacking the prescribed formalities, namely, the presence of the pastor or duly delegated priest and two witnesses), would not be recognized as valid in the eyes of the Church. Where the *Tametsi* was not published, such a union would be valid, even without the observance of sacred rites.[8] If it should eventuate that two Catholics desirous of marriage should not be able to find a parish priest or bishop within their reach, and such a condition were to last for a month, in such cases consent expressed before two witnesses would suffice for a valid marriage.[9] Thus in danger of death, or in communities isolated from the ministrations of a priest, two Catholics might exercise their natural right to marry, even though it were impossible to fulfill the formal requisites demanded by positive ecclesiastical law. All this would be done in accord with the law of the Church, though civil law might term such a union clandestine, or common law marriage. This permission of the Church has been extended even to the present day.[10]

Per se, heretics and schismatics would also be bound to observe the provisions of the *Tametsi,* for as baptized persons they come within the pale of the Church's legislative jurisdiction.[11] Yet

---

forth this work will be cited Coll. S. C. P. F.) S. C. de Prop. Fide (*C. P. pro Sin.-Tunk. Occid.*), 5 apr. 1785—*Ius Pontificium de Propaganda Fide* (ed. R. deMartinis, pars I, 7 vols., Romae, 1888-1898, pars II, Romae, 1909), Vol. I, pars II, n. 573. (Henceforth this work will be cited *Ius Pontificium.*)

8 S. C. de Prop. Fide (*C. P. pro Sin.-Tunk Occid.*), 5 apr. 1785—*Ius Pontificium,* I, pars 2, n. 573.

9 S. C. de Prop. Fide, 13 iun., 1625—*Ius Pontificium,* I, pars 2, n. 15.

10 Instr. S. C. de Prop. Fide, 1785—*Coll. S. C. P. F.*, n. 571; S. C. Concilii, decr. *Ne Temere,* 3 aug. 1907, art. VII, VIII—*Codicis Iuris Canonici Fontes cura Emi. Petri Card. Gasparri Editi* (9 vols., Romae [postea Civitate Vaticana]: Typis Polyglottis Vaticanis, 1932-39, vols. VII, VIII, IX ed. cura et studio Emi. Iustiniani Card. Seredi), n. 4340; (Henceforth this work will be cited *Fontes*); Can. 1098.

11 C. 7: "If anyone saith, that the baptized are, by baptism itself, made debtors but to faith alone, and not to the observance of the whole law of Christ; let him be anathema."

C. 8: "If anyone saith that the baptized are freed from all the precepts, whether written or transmitted, of holy Church, in such wise that they are not bound to observe them, unless they have chosen of their own accord to

with the spread of heresy becoming more rapid and extensive, and with the Catholic religion proscribed in some places, the Holy See realized that unless some exemptions were granted to heretics, numerous invalid marriages would arise. Wherefore, the following policy was, in general, adopted:

(a) In those regions wherein the *Tametsi* was never published, marriages of heretics, contracted without the prescribed form, were valid.[12]

(b) In regions where the Catholic religion prevailed, and where heretics comprised but a minority, such heretics were bound, if the *Tametsi* was in force in that region.[13]

(c) In regions where heretical religions were formed into distinct religions, with their own ministers, such heretics were not bound, since in such cases the *Tametsi* was adjudged to be extended only to Catholics.[14]

Such, in general, was the status of clandestine marriages when, in 1907, the decree *Ne temere* was issued.

ARTICLE 2. FROM THE DECREE NE TEMERE TO THE CODE OF CANON LAW

Originating in the Sacred Congregation of the Council, the

---

submit themselves thereunto; let him be anathema."—Conc. Trident., sess. VII, *de bapt;* Waterworth, *op. cit.*, 56.

[12] S. C. Conc., 18 ian. 1663 (*Ad Ep. Tricarien.*)—*Coll. S. C. P. F.*, n. 149; *Ius Pontificium*, I, pars 2, n. 142.

[13] S. C. Conc., 18 ian. 1663 (*Ad Ep. Tricarien.*)—*Coll. S. C. P. F.*, n. 149; S. C. S. Officii, 23 nov. 1898 (*Ad Ep. de Costa Rica*)—*Acta Sanctae Sedis* (41 vols., Romae, 1865–1908), XXXII (1898), 407. (Henceforth this work will be cited *ASS.*)

[14] *Declaratio Bened. PP. XIV*, 4 nov. 1741—*Coll. S. C. P. F.*, n. 333; *Bullarium Ssmi. Domini Nostri Benedicti XIV* (4 ed., 4 vols., Venetiis, 1878), I, 111, §2. That this *Declaratio* was an interpretation of the law of the Church, and therefore applicable in other similar cases, was stated by a letter of Pope Pius VII, June 27, 1805, to the Emperor Napoleon. This letter is reproduced in Artaud de Montor, *Histoire du Pape Pie VII* (2 vols., Louvain, 1836), II, ch. VI, pp. 56–57. Cf. also DeBecker, *Praelectiones canonicas de Sponsalibus et Matrimonio* (2 ed., 2 vols., Lovanii, 1903), II, 124–129; Pii X, decr. "*Provida sapientique*," 18 ian. 1906—*ASS*, XXXIX (1906–7), 81; *Analecta Ecclesiastica* (Romae, 1893–1911), XIV (1906), 149 b; Wernz, *Jus Decretalium*, IV, 246–256; Joyce, *Christian Marriage*, 130–136.

decree *Ne temere* received Papal approval on August 2, 1907, to become effective law on Easter Sunday, April 19, 1908.[15]

By the terms of this decree all Catholics of the Latin rite, when marrying among themselves, would be bound to enter marriage before two witnesses and either the parish priest or the Ordinary of the place wherein the marriage takes places, or a priest delegated by one or the other. Catholics would likewise be so bound when marrying a non-Catholic, whether baptized or not, unless for some particular place the Holy See should decide otherwise.[16]

Since this law was a disciplinary measure intended for the Latin Church, Orientals were not bound by its provisions except when they entered marriage with a Latin Catholic.[17] Thus Orientals when marrying among themselves, or when marrying any person other than a Latin Catholic, would still remain under the Tridentine legislation. An exception was made to this rule whereby Greek Ruthenians in Galicia, the United States, Canada and South America were subjected to the provisions of the *Ne temere.* The Ruthenians, in at least some of the provinces of Galicia, had observed the *Ne temere* when it was issued; prior to the declaration that Orientals were not bound by the decree, their bishops had put it in force, a practice which received the approval of the Holy See.[18] The Greek Ruthenians of Canada were declared under the discipline of the *Ne temere* in 1913;[19] those in the United States the following year,[20] and those in South America in 1916.[21]

---

[15] S. C. C., decr. *Ne temere,* 2 aug. 1907—*Fontes,* n. 4340; *ASS,* XL (1907), 527; *Analecta Ecclesiastica,* XV (1907), 320.

[16] S. C. Conc., decr. *Ne temere,* art. XI, §2—*ibid.*

[17] S. C. Conc., *Romana et aliarum,* 1 feb. 1908, ad 1 um—*Fontes,* n. 433; *ASS,* XLI (1908), 288.

[18] S. C. de Prop. Fide Pro Negotiis Ritus Orientalis, 21 maii 1911—*Archiv für katholisches Kirchenrecht* (Innsbruck, 1857–1861; Mainz, 1862–), XCII (1911), 484. (Henceforth this work will be cited *AKKR.*)

[19] Decret. S. C. de Prop. Fide pro Neg. R. O., 19 aug. 1913, art. 36—*Acta Apostolicae Sedis,* Commentarium Officiale (Romae [Civitate Vaticana], 1909–), V (1903), 398. (Henceforth this work will be cited *AAS.*)

[20] Decret. S. C. de Prop. Fide pro Neg. R. O., 17 aug. 1914, art. 30—*AAS,* VI (1904), 463.

[21] Decret. S. C. de Prop. Fide pro Neg. R. O., 27 mar. 1916, art. 17—*AAS,* VIII (1916), 107.

Latin Catholics then, and those Orientals just mentioned, cannot contract a valid clandestine, or common law marriage, but must comply with the observance of the form prescribed by the *Ne temere.*[22]

If two parties should contract marriage, one of whom is bound by the provisions of the *Ne temere,* the other exempt, the exemption of the one is not communicated to the other, according to Article XI of the decree, " unless the Holy See should decree otherwise for some particular place or region." The Holy See had declared otherwise for mixed marriages in Germany in 1906,[23] and the Holy See retained this exemption, though all others were declared void by the decree, *Ne temere.*[24] Outside of this exemption, the binding force of the decree on one party obligated both parties to the marriage to observe the form.

In summary, the clandestine marriage, or common law marriage, under the decree, *Ne temere,* would not be valid if at least one of the parties was a Catholic of the Latin rite, or of the Ruthenian Greek discipline (in those localities and since those dates listed), except in the case of impossibility to obtain the services of a priest. " Non-Catholics, whether they be baptized or unbaptized, if they marry among themselves, are in no wise bound to observe the Catholic form of betrothals or marriage." [25] Provided no other impediment existed, clandestine or common law marriages of non-Catholics, whether baptized or unbaptized, among themselves, would be valid even though no ecclesiastical form were observed.[26]

---

[22] The permission to marry without the presence of a priest when one of the parties was in danger of death, or when the impossibility to obtain a priest was present for a month, was granted by the *Ne temere;* cf. *infra,* p. 54.

[23] Pii X, decr. *Provida sapientique,* 18 ian. 1906—*AAS,* XXXIX (1906-7), 81; *Analecta Ecclesiastica,* XIV (1906), 149 b.

[24] S. C. Conc., *Romana et aliarum,* 28 mar. 1908, ad IVum et Vum—*ASS,* XLI (1908), 288; *Fontes,* n. 4349. Cf. Gasparri, *Tractatus Canonicus de Matrimonio,* ed. nova ad mentem Codicis I. C. (2 vols., [Civitate Vaticana]: Typis Polyglottis Vaticanis, 1932), n. 1019.

[25] S. C. Conc., decr. *Ne temere,* art. XI, §3—*Fontes,* n. 4340.

[26] For the diriment effects of civil legislation on the marriages of unbaptized, cf. *infra,* chapter VI, esp. p. 75.

CHAPTER V

Common Law Marriage and Baptized Persons

ARTICLE 1. LEGISLATIVE COMPETENCY OVER MARRIAGES OF THE BAPTIZED

Canon 1016 states the general principle: "The marriage of baptized persons is regulated not only by the divine law, but also by Canon Law, saving the competency of the civil power over the merely civil consequences of marriage." The divine law, whether the natural law imbedded in the hearts of men or the divine positive law promulgated by Christ, binds essentially in the same degree on all men, whether baptized or unbaptized.[1] As regards the determination of the divine law for marriage, the supreme authority of the Church alone has the right authentically to declare in what cases the divine law forbids or annuls a marriage.[2] In declaring the manner in which marriage is restricted by the divine law the Church makes use of her power of teaching, the *potestas magisterii* which Christ commissioned to her. This power of teaching belongs exclusively to the Church nor can civil power abuse or prohibit her right to exercise it. For "the Lord Jesus Christ confided to the Church the deposit of faith, in order that she, with the perpetual assistance of the Holy Ghost, may faithfully preserve and expound the revealed doctrine. The Church has independently of any civil power the right and duty

[1] Cappello, Felix M., *Tractatus Canonico-Moralis De Sacramentis,* Vol. III, *De Matrimonio* (ed. quarta emendata et aucta, Romae: apud Aedes Univ. Gregorianae, 1939), n. 56; Cathrein, Victor, *Philosophia Moralis,* ed. decima quinta (*Cursus Philosophicus,* pars VI, Friburgi Brisgoviae: Herder & Co., 1929), n. 209, p. 153.

[2] C. 1016, §1.

to teach all nations the evangelical doctrine; and all are bound by divine law to learn this doctrine, and to embrace the true Church of God." [3]

By the natural law there is demanded that the man and woman entering marriage have sufficient knowledge of the nature of marriage, and freedom of will to give mutual matrimonial consent. This consent is the constitutive element of the matrimonial contract,[4] and provided the parties be not impeded by any impediment of the divine law, natural or positive, or of competent human law, once true matrimonial consent be exchanged between the parties, the marriage is effected.

Concerning the human authority which is competent to regulate marriage, the words of canon 1012 state the principle which holds for the marriages of baptized persons: "Christ the Lord Himself raised the matrimonial contract among baptized people to the dignity of a Sacrament. Wherefore among baptized persons there can be no valid marriage contract unless it is at the same time a Sacrament." This fact, that Christ raised marriage above its normally natural plane to the supernatural dignity of a Sacrament, when entered into by baptized persons, is of prime importance in determining what power is competent to legislate for such marriages. For, as Pope Leo XIII explains: "Christ, therefore, having renewed marriage to such and so great excellence, commended and entrusted all the discipline bearing on the matter to His Church. The Church always and everywhere has so used her power with reference to the marriages of Christians, that men have seen clearly how it belongs to her as of native right; not made hers by any human grant, but given divinely to her by the will of her Founder." [5] Christian history amply testifies that at all times and against every obstacle, the Church asserted and exercised this right of hers to legislate for Christian marriage; and whenever her laws were at variance with civil laws on the

---

[3] C. 1322; Chelodi, *Ius Matrimoniale* (ed. quarta, Tridenti: Libreria Moderna Editrice A. Ardesi, 1937), n. 11, p. 10.

[4] Cf. *supra*, pp. 28–30.

[5] Ep. encyc. *Arcanum Divinae,* feb. 10, 1880—*Fontes,* n. 580; English translation from *The Pope and the People* (London and Leamington, 1895), 185.

subject, she maintained her exclusive competency over the marriages of the baptized.[6]

Since civil authority concerns only those things which are primarily civil, it remains incompetent in purely spiritual things, such as the Sacraments. But since marriage, though a Sacrament among the baptized, also concerns civil society, of which it is the basis and foundation, the state is competent over those effects of marriage which are purely civil or temporal.[7] This right of the civil authority the Church recognizes and supports. " Moreover," says Pope Leo XIII, " she (the Church) is not unaware, and never calls in doubt, that the Sacrament of Marriage, being instituted for the preservation and increase of the human race, has a necessary relation to circumstances of life, which, though connected with marriage, belong to the civil order, and about which the State rightly makes strict enquiry and justly promulgates decrees." [8]

The right of the civil authority cannot be extended, however, to those effects of marriage which are intrinsically connected with, and invariably consequent upon, the marital contract. For these effects are also under the competency of the Church whenever baptized persons are concerned. Such effects are questions concerning the freedom of the parties to enter the marriage contract, the legitimacy of the offspring, and the permission of married couples to separate from each other, even though the separation be not a permanent one. Should the civil authority deny any effects intrinsically connected with the marriage contract to a marriage which the Church considers valid, it would be overstepping its competency and going contrary to the harmonious union which should characterize the relations of the spiritual and temporal authorities;[9] a relation which, in matters which are of

---

[6] Cf. chapter III, *supra*, p. 23.

[7] C. 1016.

[8] Ep. ency. *Arcanum Divinae*, feb. 10, 1880—*Fontes*, n. 580; *The Pope and the People*, p. 201.

[9] " In such arrangement and harmony is found not only the best line of action for each power, but also the most opportune and efficacious method of helping men in all that pertains to their life here, and to their hope of salvation hereafter."—*Arcanum Divinae, Fontes*, n. 580; *The Pope and the People*, p. 201.

mutual concern to both authorities, and which are intrinsically united in one marriage, demands that the competent power control the whole affair.

Thus the Church, in canon 1038, declares that "the same supreme authority (of the Church) has the exclusive right to constitute for baptized persons other impedient and diriment impediments of marriage, either by universal or particular law." [10] Nor can the distinction be made between the Sacrament and the marriage contract among the baptized, so that the Church should regulate concerning the Sacrament while the civil power should include among its laws whatever pertains to the contract of marriage. For Christ raised the very contract among Christians to the status of a Sacrament. He instituted no new external rite for marriage, for no new sign was required. There suffices for a Sacrament a visible sign, significant of and productive of grace. The marriage pact postulates an outward expression of consent by both parties and thus of its nature supposes a visible sign.[11] This outward expression of consent was accepted by our Lord as sufficient. Among mankind in general, this mutual expression of marital consent signifies the permanent state which it introduces; outside of the Catholic Church, which views marriage as a Sacrament, this is the sole significance.[12] In the light of Christ's doc-

---

[10] The word "other" in the Canon refers to the fact that earlier in the same Canon, the Church vindicated to herself the right to declare authentically in what cases the divine law forbids or annuls a marriage.

[11] "Respondeo dicendum quod, sicut ex dictis patet, conjunctio matrimonialis fit ad modum obligationis in contractibus materialibus. Et quia materiales contractus non possunt fieri nisi ibi invicem voluntatem suam verbis promant qui contrahunt, ideo oportet quod consensus matrimonium faciens verbis exprimantur, ut expressio verborum se habeat ad matrimonium, sicut ablutio ad baptismum."—*St. Thomae Aquinatis Doctoris Angelici Summa Theologica, Supplementum,* 6 vols. (Augustae Taurinorum, [s.a.]), Qu. XLV, art. 2.

[12] "The word 'marriage' signifies in the first instance, that act by which a man and woman unite for life, with the intent to discharge towards society and one another those duties which result from the union of man and wife. The act of the union having been once accomplished, the word comes afterward to denote the relation itself. . . . The contract of the parties is simply to enter into a certain status or relation."—Schouler, *A Treatise on the Law of Husband and Wife* (Boston, 1882), p. 19.

trine and the teaching of the Church, marital consent among the baptized signifies also the graces annexed to the married state.[13]

For St. Paul,[14] treating of marriage and its obligations upon the parties to the marriage, declares that marriage between Christians has for its archetype the union between Christ and His Mystical Bride, the Church; and just as Christ and the Church by reason of that union are comparable to the head and body of a single person, so too, the same comparison holds good of the union of husband and wife. Christian marriage, being a union similar to that of Christ and His Church, must be effected by grace, since the espousals by which Christ is united to His Mystical Bride are realized through grace. Thus Christian marriage is cemented by grace. Else the simile to the union of Christ and His Church is both faint and forced.[15]

Because there can be no separation of the Sacrament of Matrimony from the marital contract between baptized persons, that authority which alone is competent to regulate the Sacraments has the exclusive right to legislate for the marriage contract of Christians. Thus the authority of Christ has removed Christian marriage from the authority of civil rulers and demanded exclusive jurisdiction over it to His Church. By the eleventh century,

---

"Marriage is either a contract or a status and relation growing out of that contract. As the former it is defined, under the modern doctrine, as a civil contract to which is essential the consent of parties capable of contracting, given according to the forms prescribed by law, if any are required. As the latter, it is the civil status or personal relation of one man and one woman, united by contract and mutual consent for their joint lives, to discharge toward each other and the community the duties imposed by law on the relation of husband and wife."—Department of Commerce and Labor, *Special Reports: Marriage and Divorce*, I, 182.

[13] Joyce, *Christian Marriage*, 154.

[14] Ephes. V, 22–32.

[15] Joyce, *op. cit.*, 154; DeSmet, *De Sponsalibus et Matrimonio*, 146.

Though it is certain that Christ raised marriage to the dignity of a Sacrament, the Church has not declared the exact moment when our Lord did so. Some authors think it may have been when Christ declared the indissolubility of marriage, "What God hath joined together, let no man put asunder" (Mt. XIX, 6); others, at the marriage feast of Cana in Galilee (John, c. III); others, when Christ, appearing to His disciples after His Resurrection, talked about the Kingdom of God.—Gasparri, *De Matrimonio*, n. 35, p. 35.

the Church had developed to a large extent her canon law on marriage, a legislation drawing its fundamental principles from revealed doctrine yet incorporating many procedural mechanics from Roman civil law. From that time on, it was universally admitted throughout Europe that, when a Sacrament was concerned, civil courts lacked competency, and matrimonial legislation and adjudication pertained solely to ecclesiastical authorities. It has already been pointed out [16] that in England, when the common law first received its name, marriage was solely administered according to Church legislation, and left to her judicial determination. Wherever the Papal authority was recognized, canon law held sway; so that men not only enjoyed a common belief concerning marriage, but were subject to a single legal system in all that concerned the primary human relationship.[17] Even when the dignity of a Sacrament was denied to Matrimony in the 16th century, matrimonial cases were still entrusted to ecclesiastical courts in England, even though these courts had been declared to derive their jurisdiction from the Crown.[18]

Since the Church had the Sacramental administration entrusted to her care, it follows that not only does legislative competency in the matter belong to her, but also exclusive judicial power concerning the marriage bond of Christians. For only that power can adequately and rightly interpret laws, which is competent to make laws.[19] The Church, because fortified by divine assistance (and precluding from her centuries of human experience), in her teaching of faith and morals can assure to matrimonial legislation and adjudication that grave and dignified approach which becomes the sacramental dignity. Furthermore, the maze of conflicting marriage laws and court decisions of modern civil jurisprudence evidences the evils consequent upon

---

[16] Cf. *supra*, p. 3.

[17] Joyce, *Christian Marriage*, pp. vii, 227, 228.

[18] Beamish v. Beamish, 11 Eng. Rep. 735; Dalrymple v. Dalrymple, 161 Eng. Rep. 665.

[19] Aichner, *Compendium Iuris Ecclesiastici* (6 ed., Brixiniae, 1887), 535; Perrone, *De Matrimonio Christiano* (3 vols., Romae, 1858), II, 6, 7.

"Laws are authoritatively interpreted by the legislator and by those to whom the power of interpreting has been committed."—C. 17.

the purely civil approach to the sacred bond of sacramental marriage.[20]

Another argument for the sole competency of the Church over marriages of the baptized may be deduced in that by receiving Baptism, a person willingly enrolls himself in the Church and submits himself to her authority. For by Baptism a person becomes a subject of the Church of Christ with all the rights and duties of a Christian.[21] The supernatural regeneration of valid Baptism gives rise to ecclesiastical membership, with the ensuing rights and obligations, just as surely as does human generation effect membership in the human race with all the consequent rights and obligations of a human being.[22]

Since the Church enjoys exclusive competence over marriages of the baptized, every recipient of valid Baptism is held to obey her laws when entering marriage, unless the Church should excuse certain individuals from such observance. For the Church many times issues dispensations so that Catholics may marry, despite certain Church laws to the contrary; and, as in canon 1099, §2, exceptions are sometimes made which excuse baptized non-Catholics from observance of Church laws. Nor is a baptized person bound to observe civil decrees concerning the marriage bond in order to enter a valid marriage, for civil authority is incompetent in attempting to legislate for or adjudicate the marriages of baptized persons. The competence of Church legislation, in so far as it touches the common law marriages of Catholics and baptized non-Catholics will be treated in the following chapters.

---

20 "Now those who deny that marriage is holy, and who relegate it, stripped of all holiness, among the class of common things, uproot thereby the foundations of nature, not only resisting the designs of Providence, but so far as they can, destroying the order that God has ordained. No one should wonder, therefore, if from such insane and impious attempts there spring up a crop of evils pernicious in the highest degree both to the salvation of souls and to the safety of the commonwealth."—Ep. encyc. *Arcanum Divinae,* feb. 10, 1880—*Fontes,* n. 580; *The Pope and the People,* 193.

21 C. 87.

22 Coronata, Matthaeus Conte a, *Institutiones Iuris Canonici* (5 vols., Taurini [Italia]: Marietti, vol. III, 1933; vol. IV, 1935; vol. V, 1936; vols. I, II, 1939), I, n. 119, pp. 132–133.

ARTICLE 2. THE CATHOLIC FORM OF MARRIAGE

The Code of Canon Law prescribes that Catholics enter a formal marriage: "Those marriages only are valid which are contracted either before the pastor or the Ordinary of the place, or a priest delegated by either, and at least two witnesses, in conformity, however, with the rules laid down in the following Canons, and save for the exceptions mentioned in canons 1098 and 1099." [23] The pastor and Ordinary [24] can assist at marriages validly only: (1) Provided they have taken canonical possession of their benefice according to canons 334, §3; 1444, §1, or have entered upon their office, provided they are not excommunicated, interdicted, or suspended from office by a condemnatory or declaratory sentence of the ecclesiastical court; (2) within the limits of their territory, wherein they validly assist not only at the marriage of their subjects, but also of those persons not their subjects; (3) provided they are not forced to assist by violence or grave fear, and ask for and receive the consent of the contracting parties.[25] The pastor and Ordinary of the place who can validly assist at marriages may also give permission to another priest to witness validly marriages within the limits of his territory; but in order that the delegation or permission be valid, it must be given to a specified priest for a specified marriage, except that regularly appointed assistants may receive general delegation for any and all marriages in the parish to which they are attached.[26]

This Catholic form of marriage is obligatory, according to canon 1099, §1, for the following persons:

(1) All persons baptized in the Catholic Church, and converted to the Church from heresy or schism (even though persons of either class mentioned should afterwards have fallen away from the Church), if they contract marriage among themselves;

---

[23] C. 1094.

[24] The term "Ordinary of the place" includes, besides the Roman Pontiff, the bishop, abbot, or prelate *nullius*, and their vicars general, administrator, vicar and prefect apostolic, in their respective territories, and in case of vacancy of these offices, to those who by law or legitimate custom succeed them in office.—C. 198.

[25] C. 1095, §1.

[26] Cc. 1095, §2, and 1096.

(2) Catholics, as just described in (1), who marry non-Catholics, either baptized or unbaptized, even after the dispensation has been obtained from the impediment of disparity of cult or mixed religion;

(3) Catholics of the Oriental rite who marry persons of the Latin rite.

Catholics of the Oriental rites are not bound by the laws of the Code, except when they intermarry with a Latin Catholic, yet some Oriental Catholics are held to enter formal marriages. An attempt will be made to list here some of the Oriental rites bound by law to enter a formal marriage:

1. The Maronites are bound by the old impediment of clandestinity,[27] not by virtue of the decree *Tametsi*, but by virtue of the Provincial Synod of the Maronites, celebrated in Mount Lebanon in 1736.[28] The acts and decrees of this synod, approved by Pope Benedict XIV *in forma specifica*, assume the character of pontifical law.[29]

If Maronites have a domicile or quasi-domicile where the Tridentine decree was not published or promulgated, they are not obliged under pain of nullity to contract marriage before the proper pastor and the required witnesses.[30] Since the marriage law of the Council of Trent was never promulgated in the greater part of the United States, in general Maronites in this country

---

[27] The old impediment of clandestinity comprised failure to follow the form established by the decree "*Tametsi*" of the Council of Trent; cf. pp. 35, 36, *supra*.

[28] "Nullum est matrimonium clandestinum, id est, quod aliter contrahitur, quam praesente parocho vel sacerdote de ipsius parochi vel ordinarii licentia et duobus vel tribus testibus."—Acta et Decreta Synodi prov. Maronit. in monte Lebano celebrata anno 1736, pars II, cap. XI, n. XII—*Acta et Decreta Sacrorum Conciliorum Recentiorum, Collectio Lacensis* (7 vols., Friburgi, Brisgoviae, 1870–1890), II, 176. (Hereafter this work will be cited as *Coll. Lac.*)

[29] Const. *Singularis*, 1 sept. 1741, §10—*Coll. Lac.* II, 488, sqq. Cf. also Duskie, John Aloysius, *The Canonical Status of the Orientals in the United States* (The Catholic University of America Canon Law Studies, n. 48; Washington: The Catholic University of America, 1928), pp. 158–162; Cappello, Felix M., *Tractatus Canonico-Moralis de Sacramentis*, Vol. III, *De Matrimonio* (4 ed., Romae: Apud Aedes Univ. Gregorianae, 1939), 481.

[30] Chelodi, *Jus Matrimoniale*, n. 139, p. 174; Duskie, *op. cit.*, 161.

could validly marry among themselves without the observance of a determined canonical form. In those places, however, where the decree "*Tametsi*" was promulgated, it seems that the form of marriage decreed by the "*Tametsi*" must be observed.[31]

2. Italo-Greeks are ruled by the law of the *Tametsi* decree of the Council of Trent, and are, therefore, held to a formal marriage under penalty of invalidity.[32] In the United States, Italo-Greeks are governed by the principles of Tridentine law as explained for the Maronites.[33]

3. The marriage of Melchites will be invalid unless celebrated with the blessing of the bishop or pastor, or a priest delegated by one or the other.[34]

4. Ukrainian Greeks, or Greek-Ruthenians, are bound by the provisions of the decree "*Ne temere,*" which was extended to those in the province of Galicia in 1911, to those in Canada August 19, 1912, to those in the United States on August 17, 1914, and those in South America on March 27, 1916.[35]

5. Syrians, Copts of the Alexandrine discipline, and Armenians have the impediment of clandestinity established by particular synodal legislation.[36]

The other Oriental disciplines observe neither the old nor the new church law requiring the formal marriage for validity.

For all Oriental Catholics, who are held to observe the formalities of marriage, any attempted common law marriage would be

---

[31] Duskie points out that some Oriental authorities maintain that the blessing of a priest is required only for the lawfulness, not for the validity of Oriental marriages. While this opinion is in theory sound, the author continues, in practice it seems that the question must be solved by an appeal to the immemorial observance of the Oriental law or custom which considers the priestly blessing necessary for validity. Duskie, *op. cit.*, 154, 155.

[32] Bened. XIV, const. "*Etsi pastoralis,*" 26 maii, 1742, #VIII—*Bullarium Pontificium Sacre Congregationis De Propaganda Fide* (6 vols., Romae, 1839-1868), III, 39; *Fontes,* n. 328.

[33] S. C. C., 1 feb. 1908, ad I—*ASS,* XLI (1908), 108, 109.

[34] Synodus nation. Melchitarum (1806), cap. IX, can. 9—Mansi, XLVI, 764; Conc. Patr. Hierosolm. (1849), cap. VII, can. 6, n. 9—Mansi, XLVI, 1056; Cappello, *De Matrimonio,* pars 2, n. 925, p. 481.

[35] Cf. *supra,* p. 39; *AKKR,* XCII (1912), 484.

[36] Cappello, *op. cit.,* 481-482.

invalid, unless they had received a dispensation from the law requiring a formal marriage, or unless by the exceptions mentioned in canon 1098, they would not have to observe the formalities as decreed by law.

ARTICLE 3. CASES WHEREIN CATHOLICS ARE EXEMPT FROM THE FORM OF MARRIAGE

Thus far the law of the Code governing the marriages of Catholics under ordinary circumstances has been treated. Foreseeing exceptional circumstances which might and actually do arise, the legislator has decreed an exemption from the form of marriage for Catholics in such circumstances by decreeing: "If the pastor or Ordinary, or a priest delegated by either, according to canons 1095 and 1096, cannot be had or if the parties cannot go to him without great inconvenience, the following rules are to be observed:

1. In danger of death marriage may be validly and licitly contracted in the presence only of two witnesses; even apart from the danger of death marriage may be contracted without the presence of an authorized priest, if it can be prudently foreseen that this state of affairs, namely, the difficulty to have an authorized priest witness the marriage, will continue for a month.

2. In either case, if there is another priest, not delegated, who can be present, he should be called and together with the witnesses assist at the marriage, though a marriage contracted only in the presence of witnesses is valid.[37]

This canon affirms the old adage: "No one is held to do the impossible," [38] and recognizes the precedence of man's natural right to marry over his duty to observe a positive law, which because of circumstances of time and place has become impossible of fulfillment.[39] In the exceptional circumstances wherein a proper priest (namely, the pastor, Ordinary of the place, or a

---

[37] C. 1098.

[38] "Nemo ad impossible tenetur."—*Reg.* 8, R. J. in VIo.

[39] Lex divina positiva et humana non obligant generatim cum incommodo valde gravi, seu cum gravi nocumento, quod per accidens observationi legis conjunctum sit,—Sabetti, Aloysio et Barrett, Timotheus, *Compendium Theologiae Moralis* (ed. tricesima tertia, New York and Cincinnati: Frederick Pustet Co., Inc., 1931), n. 86, p. 88.

priest duly delegated by one of them) could not be had, or the parties could not go to him without serious inconvenience, marriage would be valid before witnesses only. Usually it will be possible for any priest nearby to obtain proper delegation to assist at the marriage, or it will be possible for the parties to go to a proper priest. The parties would be bound to suffer some inconvenience in order to proceed according to the intended formal marriage of the Church, though if the inconvenience became serious, the form of marriage prescribed in canon 1098 may be used.[40] In modern times of facile travel, a journey by train or automobile can be made many times without serious inconvenience; if such be the case, the parties would be bound to go to a proper priest rather than contract marriage before witnesses alone.

The impossibility to obtain a proper priest, or go to him for the marriage does not necessarily mean that there must be no priest in the particular region where the parties are. Such was demanded under the rule of the "*Ne temere,*" [41] but is no longer necessary under the Code, which necessitates only a personal impossibility. Such a case might arise when a priest is impeded from calling in the pastor, or seeking his delegation, for fear of breaking the confessional seal.[42] Or again, the pastor or Ordinary of the place might be nearby, or even present materially, yet prevented by civil law from assisting at the marriage under pen-

[40] The Pontifical Commission for the Interpretation of the Code replied in reference to canons 1044 and 1045, §3, that recourse is considered impossible if telegraph or telephone are the only available means of recourse.—*ASS,* XIV, 662; Bouscaren, *Canon Law Digest* (2 vols., and Supplement-1941, Milwaukee: The Bruce Publishing Co., 1934), I, 502. Yet, Nau points out that in our country such means are extraordinary only by a great stretch of the imagination, and that prudence dictates that any manner whatsoever should be used to obtain, if possible, the presence of a proper priest at the marriage ceremony; however, since we deal here with technicalities of law, one is not bound to use the telephone, telegraph, or similarly, any extraordinary means of travel. Cf. Nau, *Manual on the Marriage Laws of the Code of Canon Law* (2nd revised ed., New York and Cincinnati: Frederick Pustet Co., Inc., 1934), n. 47, p. 59.

[41] S. C. C., decr. "*Ne temere,*" 2 aug. 1907, art. VIII—*Fontes,* 4340; *ASS,* XL (1907), 527.

[42] *Il Monitore Ecclesiastico* (Romae, 1876-), Vol. XXXII (1910), 137.

alty of heavy fine, or other similar serious inconvenience. Thus in the United States the following cases could arise wherein the pastor would be hindered from assisting at a marriage because such marriages, though permissible under the law of the Church, would be against civil law; in such cases, the assistance of the pastor would leave him liable to severe fines: (1) Two first cousins, having obtained a dispensation from the ecclesiastical impediment of affinity; (2) persons of different races, perfectly free to marry under Church law, yet impeded by a civil impediment forbidding interracial marriages;[43] (3) minors, who are free to marry without parental consent, according to Church law, as often as the parents unreasonably oppose their marriage,[44] yet hindered by civil law from marrying without parental consent, even though the refusal of that consent be unreasonable.

In each of these cases, or in any others which might arise, the pastor, Ordinary of the place, or properly delegated priest might be physically present, yet because of the serious inconvenience which prevents his assistance at the marriage, a marriage according to canon 1098 would be valid and licit. Thus the Pontifical Commission for the Interpretation of the Code has replied, though a previous response had decreed that canon 1098 referred to the physical absence of the proper priest.[45]

The first circumstance in which marriage would be valid before witnesses alone, under canon 1098, is when the danger of death is present for at least one of the contracting parties. This danger of death must no longer be imminent, as was demanded by the "*Ne temere*"; nor is there any longer required that there exist a cause, such as the securing of peace of conscience or the

---

[43] This is not meant to imply that the civil power has authority to establish diriment or impeding impediments for baptized Catholics, but merely to show that the existence of the civil law would impede a priest from assisting at the marriage unless he wished to become liable for the penalties decreed by civil law for anyone assisting at such marriages.

[44] Cf. c. 1034.

[45] Pontifical Commission for the Interpretation of the Code, resp. 25 iulii, 1931, *AAS*, XXIII, 388; Bouscaren, *Canon Law Digest*, I, 542. (Henceforth, replies to this Commission will be cited *PCI.*) Also, *PCI*, 10 martii, 1928, *AAS*, XX, 120; Bouscaren, *op. cit.*, I, 542.

legitimation of children, nor the presence of an undelegated priest, such as was formerly the case.[46]

Under the Code, any probable danger of death suffices, whether the danger arise from an internal cause, such as disease, or from an external cause, such as war, an earthquake, the danger of an impending surgical operation, etc. The same norms may be applied here as are used to determine the danger of death sufficient to allow the administration to Extreme Unction or Holy Viaticum.[47]

The second circumstance envisaged in canon 1098 is that wherein, even apart from the danger of death, it is prudently foreseen that the impossibility of obtaining or going to the proper priest will endure for a period of one month. Here again, there is a slight change from the law of the "*Ne temere*," which demanded that the impossibility of obtaining the proper priest actually exist before a marriage without the pastor, or Ordinary of the place, or properly delegated priest, would be valid.[48] Were it foreseen that the proper priest could be had within a month, even though it meant deferring the marriage for over three weeks, the use of canon 1098 would, under such circumstances, be both illicit and invalid. The month should be computed according to the prescription of canon 34, §3, 3° and 4°, though, as Doheny points out, the cases are rare when the absence of a priest can be computed with mathematical exactitude, unless there be a question of his arrival by boat, or some similar mode of conveyance with a determined schedule.[49]

Does the use of canon 1098 permit a common law marriage for

---

[46] "Imminente mortis periculo ubi parochus locive Ordinarius, aut sacerdos ab eis delegatus coram quo matrimonium celebrari queat, haberi nequeat, ad consulendum conscientiae (et si casus ferat) legitimationi prolis, matrimonium contrahi valide et licite potest coram quolibet sacerdote et duobus testibus."—S. C. C., decr. *Ne temere,* 2 aug. 1907, art. VII—*Fontes,* n. 4340; *ASS,* XL (1907), 527.

[47] Payen, *De Matrimonio in Missionibus et Potissimum in Sinis Tractatus Practicus et Casus* (2 ed., 3 vols., Zi-ka-wei: In typographia T'ou-sè-wè, 1935–1936), II, n. 1815, p. 216.

[48] S. C. C., decr. *Ne temere,* 2 aug. 1907, art. X—*Fontes,* n. 4340; *ASS,* XL (1907), 527.

[49] Doheny, *Canonical Procedure in Matrimonial Cases* (Milwaukee: The Bruce Publishing Company, 1938), 676.

Catholics? As a rule, no. The canon expressly requires the use of witnesses and, whenever possible, the presence of a priest, even though he lack the proper delegation. If a priest assisted, the marriage would not be a common law marriage, but rather a formal marriage celebrated according to the norms of the canon law for exceptional cases. And even though the priest be not present, and the marriage contracted merely before witnesses, the Church wishes the marriage to be a formal one, in that she has suggested the procedure to be followed: "If it be impossible to go before a missionary, and if there exists an urgent necessity to contract marriage, provided there be no other impediment present, let the parents in such a case choose two witnesses, who together with the bride and the groom and their relatives, should go to the church, and there, kneeling, let them recite together the usual acts of faith, hope, love and contrition, and thus let the bride and groom correctly dispose themselves for marriage. After these prayers, the bride and groom shall arise, and in the presence of the aforementioned witnesses, express to each other their consent in words of present tense, and then after returning thanks to God, let them return home. If they are unable to go to a church, let them observe the aforementioned ceremonies at home. When later the opportunity presents itself, the newly wedded couple should go before a missionary, so that he may be informed that the marriage has been correctly celebrated, and so that the couple may receive his blessing."[50] It is true that this letter, since it was directed to particular communities, does not bind the faithful at large throughout the world, yet it serves as a

[50] "Si missionarius adiri nequeat et ineundi matrimonii urgeat necessitas, atque aliunde nullum omnino obstet impedimentum, tali casu parentes duos testes eligant, qui, una cum sponso et sponsa eorumque propinquis ad ecclesiam se conferentes, flexis genibus, consuetos fidei, spei, caritatis, contritionis actus in communi recitant, sicque sponsus et sponsa ad contrahendum matrimonium recte se disponant. Post haec surgentes sponsus et sponsa coram praedictis testibus per verba de praesenti mutuum exprimant consensum, et post actas gratias Deo, domum revertantur. Si autem ad ecclesiam ire nequeant, in privatis domibus praedicta observentur. Postea, data opportunitate, novi conjuges et testes missionarium adeant, ut ipsi de matrimonio rite inito legitime constet, et ab eodem benedictionem accipiant." —S. C. de Prop. Fide, *epist. encyc. ad Epp. et Vic. Apos. in Sinis, Tungkino, Concina,* 23 iunii, 1830—*Coll. S. C. P. F.,* I, n. 816.

directive norm for those who seek to follow out the wishes of the Church, even when such wishes may not be obligatory.

If it were impossible to obtain a priest as canon 1098 desires, a common law marriage would be valid. However, if possible to obtain as one of the two witnesses required by the canon, a witness who is authorized by civil law to declare the marriage civilly valid, Catholics should attempt to secure such a person as one of the witnesses. For civil laws which look to the civil effects of marriage are binding upon all subjects, inasmuch as it is within the power of civil government to legislate concerning the civil effects of marriage.[51] And since to flaunt civil laws when it is possible to obey them, is to act against legitimate authority, it would be a sin to neglect to call in an authorized civil witness, or to fail to go before one, if it were possible *sine grave incommodo* for those marrying according to the terms of canon 1098.[52] Were it impossible to secure an authorized civil witness for the marriage according to canon 1098, a common law marriage before two witnesses would be valid for two Catholics, even though the civil laws of the place did not recognize the validity of such unions. For to deny validity to such unions contracted according to the law of the Church would be beyond the scope of civil authority.

Should the case ever arise wherein it would be impossible to have neither the priest nor two witnesses at the marriage (which would seldom, if ever, happen), marriage would be valid if entered into before only one witness, or even without witnesses, since in such circumstances the ecclesiastical law would cease to bind, because the natural law which gives to every man the right to marry, would supersede.[53]

If two Catholics had been dispensed from observing the law of the Church as to the form of marriage, common law marriage for them would be valid; but here again it must be said that there exists upon them the obligation to observe the formalities re-

[51] For baptized persons, civil laws could not legislate for any other than civil effects. C. 1016.

[52] Cf. Gasparri, *De Matrimonio,* II, n. 1295, p. 315; herein Gasparri mentions with praise that D'Annibale considers it a grave sin to forego the civil solemnities of marriage.

[53] Cf. Gasparri, *De Matrimonio,* II, n. 998, p. 134.

quired for the civil effects of marriage, and therefore there is an obligation for them to have a formal marriage, if possible, in the eyes of the civil law, even when it is impossible to observe the formalities demanded by the law of the Church. The obligation would not, however, carry with it the sanction of invalidity, if the civil formal marriage were not had.

ARTICLE 4. COMMON LAW MARRIAGE AND BAPTIZED NON-CATHOLICS

As there is but "one Lord, one faith, one Baptism,"[54] so too, there is but one Church set up by Christ to "teach all nations . . . all things whatsoever I have commanded you."[55] The authority of that Church, being both complete and exclusive concerning whatever is contained in her divine commission, extends not merely over Catholics, but also over all baptized persons. For, according to canon 87, "by Baptism a person becomes a subject of the Church of Christ with all the rights and duties of a Christian, unless as far as rights are concerned there is some obstacle impeding the bond of communion with the Church, or a censure inflicted by the Church."

It is readily noted that this canon declares that an obstacle impeding the bond of communion with the faithful may interfere with a person's rights. But it does not relax the duties which such persons have towards the Church. The fact that a person is in heresy or schism does not restrict or limit the legislative power of the Church so that she may not legislate for him. Those who lapse into heresy or schism are bound by all laws of the Church unless exemption is granted to non-Catholics. The same may be said of apostates.[56] Those born in heresy or schism[57]

---

[54] Ephes., IV, 4.

[55] Matt., XXVIII, 19.

[56] "Qui recenti apostasia ad castra acatholica transierunt vel incredulitatem professi sint beneficium exemptionis e sua rebellione reportare nequent."—Vermeersch-Creuzen, *Epitome Iuris Canonici,* I, n. 106, p. 103.

[57] This phrase is admittedly far from precise, since no one is born with Baptism already received; yet the phrase is commonly used to denote those children who are born of schismatic or heretical parents, and who therefore receive the heresy or schism from their first moments of educational awakening.

and educated outside of the Church may be excused from the non-observance of ecclesiastical laws on the grounds of ignorance of the laws, but such an excuse is an absolution of moral guilt rather than a juridical exemption from such laws. For the Code expressly states that "No ignorance of invalidating or inhabilitating laws excuses unless the law explicitly admits ignorance as an excuse."[58] Nor, as the same canon 16 continues, is ignorance or error concerning a law presumed in anyone. Only in the penal law of the Church does ignorance have effect as an excusing factor.[59]

However, foreseeing the difficulties which might arise if she enforced obedience to all her laws on those baptized persons who are outside of the true faith, the Church has wisely tempered the execution of her laws with consideration and mildness, so that some of the laws are limited so as to bind only on Catholics. Thus, canon 1099, §2, excuses from the observance of the Catholic form of marriage all non-Catholics baptized as well as unbaptized: "Saving the rule of §1, n. 1 (of the same Canon), non-Catholics, whether baptized or unbaptized, are nowhere held to the Catholic form of marriage when they contract marriage among themselves. Exempt also are children of non-Catholics, who, though they were baptized in the Catholic Church, were reared from their infancy in heresy or schism, or in infidelity or without any religion, when they contract marriage with non-Catholics." The marriage of a Catholic with a non-Catholic remains regulated by paragraph 1 of that canon, and is subject to the Catholic form prescribed in canon 1094.

Upon being asked concerning the interpretation of the phrase "children of non-Catholics," the Pontifical Commission for the Interpretation of the Code replied that this phrase included also the children born of parents, only one of whom is a non-Catholic, the other parent being a Catholic,[60] as well as the children born of apostates.[61] The interpretation, given in 1929, was said to be a

[58] C. 16, §1.

[59] Cf. c. 2229.

[60] *PCI,* 20 iulii, 1929, ad II—*AAS* (1929), XXI, 573; Bouscaren, *Canon Law Digest,* I, 543; Nau, *Manual on the Marriage Laws of the Code of Canon Law,* App. I, n. 6, pp. 220, 221.

[61] *PCI,* 17 feb., 1930—*AAS,* XXII (1930), 195; Bouscaren, *op. cit.,* I, 544.

declarative one, rather than an extensive one; therefore, by virtue of canon 17, §2, the interpretation was retroactive to the time of the promulgation of the Code, having as much force as the law itself.[62] Thus, in a case submitted by the Archdiocesan Curia of St. Louis to the Holy Office, a girl, born of a Catholic mother and a non-Catholic father, and baptized when less than a year old as a Catholic, but receiving no Catholic education whatsoever, was judged to have married validly when she married a Lutheran man before a justice of the peace. This marriage took place in 1922, which was post-Code, yet prior to the interpretation of canon 1099 given in 1929.[63]

Thus, as far as the Church law regarding a formal marriage is concerned, children born of parents, one of whom is a Catholic, the other a non-Catholic or apostate, or both of whom are non-Catholics or apostates, are, if they are baptized Catholic but receive no Catholic education, assimilated to non-Catholics, and are exempt from the prescriptions of canon 1094. Similarly they may be said to be excused from the obligations of canon 1098, since canon 1099 excludes them from the observance of "catholicam matrimonii formam." And though canon 1098 is not prescribing the full formalities of canon 1094, yet it does prescribe certain formalities which if possible of execution, are necessary for the validity of a marriage.

Another exemption granted in the Code of baptized non-Catholics may be noted in canon 1070, which restricts the impediment of disparity of cult to those baptized in the Catholic Church, or converted to it: "The marriage between a person baptized in the Catholic Church, or received into the Church from heresy or schism, and a non-baptized individual is null and void." Prior to the Code this impediment included also those marriages wherein one party was baptized, even though a non-Catholic, and

---

[62] *PCI,* 25 iulii, 1931—*AAS,* XXIII (1931), 388; Bouscaren, *op. cit.,* I, 544.

[63] The private reply of the Holy Office was given June 9, 1931, and is reported in *Periodica de Re Canonica et Morali utili Praesertim Religiosis et Missionariis* (Bruges, 1905-), XXI, 14. (Hereafter this publication will be cited *Periodica.*)

one party was unbaptized.[64] The Code makes it evident, however, that baptized non-Catholics are no longer bound by this impediment. The Holy Office in a private reply to the Archbishop of Friburg confirms this: "The impediment of disparity of cult does not apply to non-Catholics unless these were baptized in the Catholic Church or converted to the same." [65]

Under the Code, then, a common law marriage would be possible for a baptized non-Catholic and an unbaptized person,[66] as far as the Church law is concerned, provided no other impediments existed.

For though baptized non-Catholics (i.e., "those not baptized in the Catholic Church") do not come under the prescriptions of canon 1070, and though they are exempted from observing the Catholic form of marriage, they must, by virtue of canon 87, be considered as subjects of the Church law, and held by the other diriment impediments which state no exemption for heretics and schismatics.

---

[64] Benedictus XIV, epist. *Singulari Nobis,* 9 febr. 1749—*Fontes,* II, n. 394. ". . . invalidum est matrimonium contractum inter baptizatum et infidelem etiamsi pars baptizata sit haeretica vel schismatica vel apostata, vel pars infidelis sit catechumena vel bona fide credatur baptizata."—Feije, *De Impedimentis et Dispensationibus Matrimonialibus* (ed. secunda, Lovanii, 1874), n. 459, p. 325. Cf. also Gasparri, *De Matrimonio,* n. 566, p. 350.

[65] This reply, never published in the *AAS,* may be seen in *AKKR,* CV (1925), 202; Bouscaren, *Canon Law Digest,* I, 512; Sartori, *Enchiridion Canonicum* (ed. sexta, Vicetiae: Ex Typographia Commerciali, 1938), 238. A reply of the Sacred Congregation for the Propagation of the Faith, 26 febr. 1924, is of the same tenor: "Per hanc primam huius canonis paragraphum ita mutatum est ius vetus, ut in novo iure haeretici extra Ecclesiam catholicam baptizati et numquam ad eamdem conversi, etiamsi sine dispensatione, validum contrahunt matrimonium cum parte non baptizata."—Sartori, *Enchiridion Canonicum,* 238.

[66] Those who have been "baptized in the Catholic Church" would be bound by the impediment. For a treatment as to who may be considered to be baptized in the Catholic Church, cf. *Jus Pontificium* (Romae, 1921–), V (1925), 162–163; Hilling, "Neueste Entscheidungen des Hl. Stuhles über das Ehehindernis der Religionsverschiedenheit, die Auflösung einer Naturehe und die Anwendung des Privilegium Paulinum."—*AKKR,* CVII (1927), 178–186, esp. 180–181; Schenk, *The Matrimonial Impediments of Mixed Religion and Disparity of Cult* (The Catholic University of America Canon Law Studies, n. 51, Washington, D. C.: The Catholic University of America, 1929), 103–112.

" Per se etiam ipsi adstringuntur legibus ecclesiasticis in genere cum sint subditi Ecclesiae, licet rebelles et transfugae, nisi Ecclesia, pia mater, ne peccata multiplicentur, velit illos eximere. . . . Sed etiam illos, qui in haeresi et schismate nati sunt, si aliis fortasse legibus Ecclesia ob rationem commiserationis ligare non intendit, vult tamen eos impedimentis matrimonialibus adstringere, excepta forma canonica et impedimento *disparitatis cultus,* de qua re alias. Id certissimum est, ac illi AA. catholici qui de hoc dubitant, nesciunt quid dicant." [67]

Baptized non-Catholics, then, can enter a marriage among themselves validly, even though civil laws do not recognize such unions as valid. For such persons, through Baptism, come under the Church's jurisdiction, and are effectively removed from civil jurisdiction as regards marriage, except concerning purely temporal matters.[68] If no ecclesiastical impediment nullifies their marriage, their common law marriage would be a Sacramental one.[69]

---

[67] Gasparri, *De Matrimonio,* I, n. 257, pp. 161–162; cf. also Chelodi, *Ius Matrimoniale,* n. 37, p. 38; n. 138, p. 173.

[68] Cf. article 1 in this chapter.

[69] The discussion of the validity of a common law marriage between a baptized non-Catholic and an unbaptized person in those states or territories which do not admit common law marriage will be reserved until the authority of the state to legislate for non-baptized persons has been treated.

CHAPTER VI

Common Law Marriage and Unbaptized Persons

Article 1. Competent Legislative Power over Marriages of the Unbaptized

Common law marriage among the unbaptized is naturally expected to be more frequent than among the baptized. For Christianity, whose initiation ceremony is the Sacrament of Baptism, has given to the world the sacred concept of marriage with its attendant and significant formalities. Yet, marriage even among the unbaptized is something sacred by its very nature,[1] and is governed by laws. An examination of marriage may consider it as being under a triple jurisdiction, that of the natural law, the ecclesiastical law, and civil law.

The natural law governs all men. Common law marriage, then, among the unbaptized is subject to all the prescriptions and prohibitions of the natural law. For, as St. Thomas Aquinas points out,[2] marriage belongs under the natural law because human nature inclines itself to marriage in a twofold manner: First, inasmuch as the principal end or purpose of marriage is the propagation of the human race, the procreation of children and their education to the perfect status of manhood; secondly, inasmuch as the secondary end of marriage is the mutual aid and complement which husband and wife render each other in their domestic life.[3] Common law marriages among the unbaptized must consequently conform to the natural law, or else be adjudged no marriages at all.

---

[1] Pope Leo XIII, encyclical letter, *Arcanum Divinae,* 10 febr., 1880—*Fontes,* n. 580.

[2] "Matrimonium de jure naturae, vel naturale est, non quia sit a natura, sed quia ad ipsum propter bonum prolis et mutuum fidele obsequium maxime natura inclinat."—IIa IIae, q. XLI, art. 1.

[3] There natural ends of marriage are recognized in canon 1013.

In determining the binding power of ecclesiastical law on common law marriage among the unbaptized, the former must be considered with this distinction in mind: Some Church laws declare those principles wherein the natural or divine positive law forbids or annuls a marriage, while other Church laws go beyond the natural and the divine positive law to declare merely ecclesiastical impediments to marriage. In declaring the divine law which forbids or prohibits a marriage, the Church is but carrying out her divine commission to preserve and to pass on to all men the divine teaching. This power implies the exercise of her office of teaching, which extends to all mankind: "The Church has independently of any civil power the right and the duty to teach all nations the evangelical doctrine; and all are bound by divine law to learn this doctrine, and to embrace the true Church of God." [4] Inasmuch as the unbaptized are subject to the divine law, whether it be the natural law or the divine positive law, they must observe the impediments which, though set up by the divine law, require to be authentically declared by the supreme authority of the Church. For "the supreme authority of the Church alone has the right to declare authentically in what cases the divine law forbids or annuls a marriage." [5]

As regards the unbaptized, the divine law binds concerning: the ends of marriage; its essential properties, namely, unity and indissolubility; the diriment impediments of impotency and previous marriage (*ligamen*); in some degree the impediment of consanguinity; the necessity of true consent; and the separation of the married parties.[6]

As to the binding force of other laws of the Code, in general and in reference to common law marriages among the unbaptized, canon 12 states the general principle: "Unbaptized persons are not held to laws which are purely Church laws . . ." The Church has never considered the unbaptized as *direct* subjects of

---

[4] C. 1322, §2. Cf. DeSmet, *De Sponsalibus et Matrimonio,* n. 426, pp. 366, 367.

[5] C. 1038, §1.

[6] Payen, *De Matrimonio,* I, n. 190, p. 138; also canons 1013, 1068, 1069, 1076, 1081–1087, 1092–1093, 1111, 1118.

her legislation.[7] St. Paul admitted this principle when he wrote to the Corinthians: "What have I to do to judge them that are without?"[8] St. Thomas Aquinas, in commenting on these words, teaches that the Apostle herein speaks about pagans and infidels who have not the Baptismal character by which they become affiliated with the Church.[9] Consistently the Church has considered unbaptized persons as not being subject to merely ecclesiastical laws.[10]

If the Church, then, holds herself incompetent to pass a law decreeing the necessity of a formal marriage among the unbaptized (for this would be to bind the unbaptized *directly*), marriages among the unbaptized either remain solely under the divine law, or else are governed also by civil authority.

For a long time the competency of civil authority over the marriages of the unbaptized remained unquestioned. Prior to 1780, the unanimous opinion of canonists and theologians agreed that civil authority could legislate for the natural contract of marriage among the unbaptized, just as it could for other contractual obligations which men undertake.[11] In fact, some authors, over-

[7] As to the *indirect* subjection of an infidel to Church marriage laws, cf. *infra*, Ch. VI, article 2.

[8] I Cor., V, 12.

[9] "*Ad primum* ergo dicendum quod Apostolus loquitur de paganis et aliis infidelibus qui non habent characterem, per quem annumerati sunt populi Dei."—*Suppl.*, q. XXII, art. 6, ad 1.

[10] C. 8, X, *de divortiis*, IV, 19; Conc. Trident., sess. XIV, *de poenitentia*, c. 2; Benedictus XIV, ep. *Singulari*, 9 febr. 1749—*Fontes*, n. 394. In commenting on this point in canon 12, Cicognani declares: "The Code canonized this principle in canon 87. This Canon decrees that by Baptism a human being becomes a *person* in the Church of Christ. However, valid Baptism is required; nor does putative Baptism suffice. To belong to the body of the Church, one must be united to the ecclesiastical society by a valid act, that is, by a real bond, since God has nowhere decreed that putative Baptism produces the same effect as valid Baptism."—Cicognani, *Canon Law*, 2nd revised edition, authorized English version by Jos. O'Hara and Francis Brennan (Philadelphia: The Dolphin Press, 1935), p. 362.

[11] Schmalzgrueber, *Ius Ecclesiasticum Universum* (5 vols. in 12, Romae, 1843–1845), lib. IV, tit. I, n. 364; Sanchez, *De Sancto Matrimonii Sacramento Disputationum Libri Decem. in Tres Tomos Distributi* (Venetiis, 1712), l. VIII, disp. III, n. 5; Wernz-Vidal, *Ius Canonicum* (7 vols. in 8, Romae; apud Aedes Universitatis Gregorianae, 1923–1938), V (2 ed., *Ius Matrimoniale*), n. 68, p. 82.

emphasizing the civil aspect of the contract of marriage, and asserting that the Sacrament of Matrimony could only accede to a valid civil contract, placed the sole competency in establishing matrimonial impediments, even among the baptized, in civil authority. They excluded the Church, which, they said, was a purely spiritual power. These Regalist writers asserted that the matter of the Sacrament of Matrimony was, as in every marriage, a valid civil contract. Without a valid contract, there could be neither marriage, nor Matrimony. And since, according to their theory, it is the exclusive right of the State to regulate all civil contracts, any ecclesiastical authority over marriage was a usurpation of civil authority, and lacked all basis of right. Thus Marcus de Dominis, an apostate archbishop writing shortly after the Council of Trent, and John Launoy, an apostate and a Lutheran, writing in the 17th century, led many other heretics in this attack on the Church's power over marriage. Their works were condemned by the Church; but their followers ranged through Austria, France, Italy and Belgium.[12]

Perhaps it was in an endeavor to counteract this heresy which placed all power of matrimonial legislation in civil authority that Catholic writers for the first time denied to civil authority all power of establishing matrimonial impediments, even for the unbaptized. First advanced [13] by DePey in 1788,[14] this theory grew very rapidly, being defended also by Muzzarelli,[15] Martin,[16] Feije,[17] Liberatore,[18] and Perrone,[19] among others.[20]

---

[12] Perrone, *De Matrimonio Christiano,* II, 33–36; Feije, *De Impedimentis et Dispensationibus Matrimonialibus,* 2, 3; Giovine, *De Dispensationibus Matrimonialibus* (2 vols., Neapoli, 1863–1866), I, 2–4; Roskovány, A. de, *Matrimonium in Ecclesia Catholica* (4 vols., Pestini [Nitriae], 1861–1881), I, 2–5.

[13] According to Wernz-Vidal, *Ius Matrimoniale,* n. 68, p. 82.

[14] *De l'autorité des deux puissances* (4 vols., Strasbourg, 1788), III, ch. 3, §8, p. 158, sqq.

[15] *Il buon uso della logica in materia di religioni* (11 vols. in 6, Firenze, 1821–1823), VII, opusc. XXIX, p. 200, sqq.

[16] *De Matrimonio ac potestate ipsum dirimendi ecclesiae soli exclusive propria* (2 vols., Lugduni, 1844), II, 2–115.

[17] *De Impedimentis et Dispensationibus Matrimonialibus,* nn. 67–70, pp. 48–51. Feije claims that the opposite opinion, though admittedly the more common one, is not sufficiently proven.

At present this theory has been adequately refuted.[21] The main points on which the above mentioned authors based their theory were: (1) Marriage is by its nature something sacred, so that it cannot come under the competency of mere civil society; (2) civil authority cannot legislate for an internal act, such as is necessary to constitute a true bond of marriage; (3) marriage pertains to the law of nature, and therefore not to civil law. The falsity of the opinion can best be demonstrated by proof of the opposite opinion which today is more common, namely, that the State has the right to legislate for the marriages of the unbaptized among themselves, even to the extent of establishing diriment impediments or invalidating laws relative to these unions.

This right of the State may be proven: (1) From a consideration of the nature of marriage, which shows that there is no repugnance to its being governed by civil authority; (2) From a consideration of the rights and duties of civil government, which shows that it should legislate for the marriages of the unbaptized; (3) From the official documents of the Holy See, which expressly declare that civil authority is competent to legislate for marriages of the unbaptized, even to the extent of setting up diriment impediments for these unions.

1. Considering the nature of marriage, it can, as has already been stated, be considered as coming under the natural, ecclesiastical or civil law. Granting the jurisdiction of the natural law, and remembering that, among the unbaptized, ecclesiastical laws do not bind directly, the question resolves itself to this: Does the nature of marriage exclude human, civil authority from legislating for that contract? The answer must be a negative one, for the nature of marriage among the unbaptized does not differ from that among the baptized. In the latter case, Christ's determination of the contract as a Sacrament deliberately places it under

---

[18] *Institutiones Philosophicae,* vol. III, *Ethica et ius naturae* (8 ed., Romae, 1855), lib. II, cap. 1, art. IV.

[19] *De Matrimonio Christiano,* II, 439–470.

[20] Cf. authors cited by Wernz-Vidal, *Ius Matrimoniale,* n. 68, p. 82, and Perrone, *op. cit.,* 460–461.

[21] Gasparri, *De Matrimonio,* I, nn. 248–251, pp. 154–159.

the exclusive competency of the Church. But both marriage among the unbaptized and marriage among the baptized are contracts; both are effected valid unions by the mutual consent of the contracting parties; both have the same restrictions of natural law as to unity and indissolubility, and in regards to the impediments of impotency, *ligamen,* and certain degrees of consanguinity.[22] Whereas both contracts are subject equally to the natural law, in both types there are many matters left undetermined by the natural law, e.g., to what degree should the impediment of consanguinity be extended? At what age should youths be allowed to enter this contract?[23] Nothing in the nature of the matrimonial contract precludes positive legislation by competent authority from extending the impediments of the natural law beyond the limits established by the natural law itself. Otherwise, the Church could not so extend these impediments. Competent authority can also positively legislate so that nullifying laws, not found in the natural law, may be brought to bear on the matrimonial contract. Were this not true, the Church could not have evolved the complete legislation which she has set up for marriage among the baptized. She determines the form for contracting marriage, and sets up impediments which are not found in the natural law, v. gr., the impediments of Sacred Orders, Solemn Vow, Abduction, Crime, Public Decency, Spiritual Relationship and Legal Relationship, all of which are diriment impediments within defined limits.[24] For the unbaptized then, the same principle must remain true, namely, that competent authority can legislate for the marriages of the unbaptized. That competent authority either does not exist, or is some established power independent from the State, or is the State itself.[25]

To say that no competent authority exists for marriages of the

---

[22] Payen, *De Matrimonio,* I, n. 190, p. 138; Quigley, *Matrimonial Impediments and Dispensations* (Philadelphia: The Dolphin Press, 1939), pp. 4, 5.

[23] The natural law demands for validity only that mental and physical age or maturity which is consonant with the undertaking of the serious obligations of marriage; beyond these limits the impediment of age, as established by the Code, is of merely ecclesiastical establishment.—Gasparri, *De Matrimonio,* I, n. 492, p. 291.

[24] Cc. 1094, 1072, 1073, 1074, 1075, 1078, 1079 and 1080.

[25] Cf. Cappello, *De Matrimonio,* n. 76, p. 88, for this same method of argumentation.

unbaptized would be to say that God, from Whom flows all power and authority, has not provided a source of supervision and guidance for the contract of marriage among the unbaptized, which, of all contracts, needs supervision and guidance. This would militate against His divine wisdom and goodness. For to provide unbaptized mankind with an authority in other natural contracts, and to omit such provision for the most important contract in man's life, would be to leave man constantly in doubt concerning his freedom to enter the marriage contract with a determined person, concerning the validity of his present marriage, concerning his rights and obligations towards his children and his fellowman. That all these details concerning marriage are not in themselves clear from the natural law itself, especially as pertaining to individual cases, may be evidenced in the huge amount of adjudication necessary to determine such questions, even among the baptized, who possess a more complete teaching and understanding of the divine teaching on marriage.

Such an authority does not exist for the unbaptized, independently from the State, for there are but two societies in the perfect sense of the word, namely, the Church and the State.[26] And within these two, the Church and the State, is man's spiritual and temporal welfare respectively and adequately cared for.[27] There has not been set up any religious society apart from the Church which might care for the spiritual needs of those outside the Church. Since then, it has been shown that it would militate against God's goodness and wisdom if a competent authority did not exist for the marriages of the unbaptized, and since there is no other such authority outside of the State, the State itself is competent to legislate for the marriages of its unbaptized citizens, marrying among themselves.[28]

Nor is that argument tenable which objects that marriage is of

[26] "Et quoniam duae solum dantur specie distinctae societates perfectae, Ecclesia et Status, sequitur omnes alias societates quae existunt in mundo necessario referri et subordinari vel Ecclesiae vel Statui prout bonum temporale vel spirituale prosequuntur."—Ottaviani, *Institutiones Iuris Publici Ecclesiastici* (ed. altera, 2 vols., Civitate Vaticana: Typis Polyglottis Vaticanis, 1935–1936), I, 64–65.

[27] Ottaviani, *op. cit.*, I, 60–61.

[28] Cappello, *De Matrimonio*, n. 76, p. 88.

its very nature so sacred that it is repugnant that it be controlled by civil authority.[29] By virtue of this same argument, civil authority would be entirely incompetent in regard to oaths, which are sacred, in fact in regard to every baptized person, who through Baptism becomes consecrated to God.[30] It must be remembered that duly constituted civil authority is sacred in the sense that the power wielded by the power of civil government comes from God, and that offenses against the just laws of civil government are not merely civil crimes, but also sins.[31]

Nor can it be validly objected that since marriage is by its nature prior to civil government, civil authority cannot legislate for it.[32] Certainly marriage historically antedated civil government, and logically marriage is the pre-existing foundation upon which the structure of the State is reared. But once civil authority is established, as happened very early in human history, it must be admitted that that government antedates all subsequent marriages, and that for those marriages civil authority is both antecedent and competent. Furthermore, man antedates civil government, yet who, would, on that ground, deny the competency of civil government over the men it governs?[33]

2. Looking at the rights and the duties of civil government, it can be seen that there exists in such government the right and duty to legislate for the marriages of its unbaptized citizens. Among the faithful, the exclusive competency of the Church precludes civil competency over the marriage bond. But for the unbaptized, unless its competency be pre-empted by a superior society, or excluded by the nature of the matter under consideration, the State has the right and the duty to legislate whenever

---

[29] Perrone, *De Matrimonio Christiano,* II, 444.

[30] Wernz-Vidal, *Ius Matrimoniale,* n. 71, p. 86.

[31] Perrone himself admits: ". . . facile assentior leges principum etiam infidelium, quod sancitae fuerint in commune societatis bonum quaeque non adversentur sive iuri naturali sive divino, obstringere subditos in conscientia, adeo ut isti nequeant illas sine peccato infringere."—*op. cit.,* II, 441. "Necessaria est auctoritati civili potestas condendi leges in conscientia obligantes."—Cathrein, *Philosophia Moralis,* Thesis XCVII, p. 490.

[32] This objection is raised by Liberatore, *Ethica et ius naturae,* lib. II, cop. I, art. IV.

[33] Gasparri, *De Matrimonio,* I, 157; Wernz-Vidal, *Ius Matrimoniale,* p. 83, *in nota.*

the public welfare demands it.[34] Since neither the Church, as a superior society, nor the nature of marriage denies this competency to civil authority, the State has the right and duty to legislate concerning the marriages of the unbaptized.

It has been objected that such legislation is a usurpation of domestic and personal authority.[35] But domestic and personal rights many times need the aid of civil authority both to augment and protect these rights, and sometimes to restrict them so that the common good of all may best be procured. This the State does by unifying marriage laws and customs among citizens of diversified nationalities and customs, just as does the Church for her subjects.[36]

Nor can it be objected that whatever specifically belongs under the natural law (*quae in individuo sunt de iure vel officio naturae*) cannot be apt matter for civil legislation; and since marriage belongs specifically under the natural law, therefore, civil law has no right to touch it. St. Thomas teaches that the natural law can be determined by positive law.[37] Just as the Church in her marriage laws complements natural laws with prescriptions and prohibitions, so, too, may the civil authority for its subjects. It must be admitted that once the marriage contract is formed, the authority of the Church or State cannot change those properties which flow from the contract by the very law of nature, such as the unity and indissolubility of marriage; but this should not militate against the argument just stated.[38]

3. From the official documents of the Holy See may be established the fact that civil authority can legislate for marriage among the unbaptized even to the extent of establishing invalidating laws or diriment impediments.

On October 29, 1739, the Sacred Congregation of the Holy Office, referring to a marriage contracted between two infidels, gave the following answer in its Instruction: "And since legiti-

[34] Cf. Gasparri, *De Matrimonio*, n. 241, pp. 146, 147.

[35] Liberatore, *loc. cit.*

[36] Gasparri, *De Matrimonio*, I, 158.

[37] "Ea quae pertinet ad legem naturae sunt determinibilia per ius positivum."—Ia IIae, q. 95, art. 2.

[38] Wernz-Vidal, *Ius Matrimoniale*, p. 83 *in nota;* Gasparri, *De Matrimonio*, n. 250, p. 156.

mate marriage entails indissolubility as its necessary condition or circumstance, only the death of one of the parties can dissolve it. Wherefore, if Titius be bound in legitimate marriage to Bertha, in paganism, with those solemnities *which, according to the laws and commonly accepted customs in China* are necessary for a legitimate marriage, the marriage bond between them shall always endure, until the death of one of the parties shall sever it." [39] Though this answer is not a direct proof of the point in question, it may be argued from this response that the Holy Office *per contrarium* agrees that the laws or commonly accepted customs in China could decree solemnities which would be necessary for validity of marriage, and thus civil authority could legislate for the very bond of marriage. Wernz-Vidal is of the opinion that the "solemnities" referred to might refer to those *signs* by which consent is manifested among the pagans; [40] but as Cappello points out, even if these "solemnities" do mean *signs* by which consent be expressed, the reference is certainly not to *signs* which according to the natural law suffice to express consent, for according to the natural law any *sign* expressive of consent would suffice, but to *signs* required by civil law or custom; and since the absence of these requisite *signs* would invalidate the marriage, the competency of civil authority is apparent.[41]

Another decree of the Holy Office was occasioned by a query submitted by the Vicar-Apostolic of Yun-nan, September 20, 1854: "In these missions it often happens that a young man marries the widow of his older brother, and is later converted. Only with difficulty can the couple be separated, either because of chil-

---

[39] ". . . E perchè il matrimonio legittimo porta seco, per condizione o circonstanza necessaria, l'indissolubilità . . . perciò solo la morte può render sciolto un tal matrimonio. Dunque se Tizio si è congiunto in legittimo matrimonio con Berta nello stato d'infedeltà *con quelle solennità, che secondo le leggi ed usi comuni della Cina* dichiarano il contratto vero e legittimo, resta sempre vivo il vincolo fra essi, se la morte di alcuno di essi non lo scioglie."—Gasparri, I, *De Matrimonio,* I, n. 245, p. 150.

[40] Wernz-Vidal, *Ius Matrimoniale,* p. 89, *in nota;* with this author Chelodi (*Ius Matrimoniale,* n. 13, p. 14) also agrees that this response lacks any probative force for the point under consideration.

[41] Cappello, *De Matrimonio,* p. 89, *in nota;* Gasparri, *De Matrimonio,* n. 245, p. 150, also agrees that this argument is valid.

dren already born of the union, or because of the danger that they might be turned against the Faith. Their marriage seems to be invalid inasmuch as it is forbidden, even under the penalty of death, by civil law. After Baptism, then, is it enough for the convalidation of their marriage that they renew their consent?" To this proposed case the Holy Office replied September 20, 1854: "Having secured a dispensation from the impediment of disparity of cult, and affinity in the first degree, through use of the faculties which the missionaries possess, the consent must be renewed. But if from this practice, some evils are foreseen, let the parties remain in good faith." [42] From this response it may be concluded that the Holy Office, inasmuch as it ordered the renewal of matrimonial consent absolutely, and not conditionally or *ad cautelam,* considered the marriage invalid, and since the only apparent grounds of invalidity is the civil impediment of affinity, the competency of the civil authority over the unbaptized may be argued.[43]

From the Congregation for the Propagation of the Faith come two documents which more clearly prove the point, and which are more unanimously accepted in that respect by canonists. An Instruction from this Congregation sent to missionaries in India, December 5, 1631, includes the following as the *sententia* of theo-

---

[42] "In istis missionibus saepe evenit, ut minor fratris sui maioris defuncti uxorem ducat, et postea convertatur. Difficillime separari possunt propter prolem iam susceptam, vel periculum ne avertantur a fide. Ipsorum matrimonium invalidum esse videtur, utpote omnino a lege civili prohibitum etiam sub poena mortis. Verum post baptismum, ad convalidandum eorum matrimonium, satisne est ut tantummodo suum renovent consensum?" Resp.: "Praevia dispensatione disparitatis cultus, et primi affinitatis gradus per facultates quibus missionarii gaudent, consensum esse renovandum. Quod si superventura mala deprehendatur, relinquendos in bona fide."—*Collectanea S. C. P. F.*, n. 1104.

[43] Gasparri, *op. cit.*, n. 245, p. 151. Cf. Cappello, *op. cit.*, 88-89, who answers the objection of Wernz-Vidal (*op. cit.*, 88) that the argument is not a peremptory one, inasmuch as it is not clear that the civil law, though a serious penal one, was incapacitating or invalidating; and furthermore that the Cardinals did not hold the opinion as certain and undoubted, but only as probable, and that their action was to make a dubiously valid marriage certainly valid. Chelodi, *Ius Matrimoniale*, n. 13, p. 14, agrees with Wernz-Vidal, without commenting on the opinion of Cappello.

logians and canonists:[44] "Polygamists of India, who together with all their wives, are converted to the Faith and baptized, must dismiss all their wives, except their first, who is the real wife, if in her marriage there was no impediment of the natural law or of the positive law laid down by their civil legislator." The express condition concerning the impediment established by civil authority argues to the competency of that authority. Payen,[45] Wernz-Vidal,[46] Gasparri[47] and Cappello[48] all agree that this document furnishes proof that the civil authority enjoys competency over the marriage bond among the unbaptized.

The second document from the Congregation for the Propagation of the Faith is one whose existence was doubted by some authors when first it was alleged as an argument in favor of civil competency.[49] However, it is a document contained in the *Collectanea S. C. P. F.*, an official publication of responses from the Society of the Propagation of the Faith, and its authenticity is accepted by leading canonists.[50] The response of the Congregation for the Propagation of the Faith has great force since it decreed the nullity of a marriage of two infidels, granting them the right to re-marry; for such a decision to be arrived at, the Congregation had to have full proof of the point in question, both as to the law governing the case and as to the facts of the case.[51]

---

[44] "Indi polygami qui cum omnibus mulieribus suis convertuntur ad fidem et baptizantur, tenentur dimittere omnes uxores praeter primam, quae sola est vera uxor, si in illius matrimonio nullum intervenit impedimentum iuris naturalis vel positivi conditi ab eorum Principe."—*Collectanea S. C. P. F.*, n. 71.

[45] *Op. cit.*, I, n. 207, p. 154, *in nota.*

[46] *Op. cit.*, n. 73, pp. 88–89.

[47] *Op. cit.*, I, n. 246, p. 151.

[48] *Op. cit.*, 90.

[49] Perrone, *De Matrimonio Christiano*, II, 468; Feije, *De Impedimentis et Dispensationibus Matrimonialibus*, 50.

[50] *Collectanea S. C. P. F.*, n. 744, and *not.* 1; Cappello, *op. cit.*, 90–91; Wernz-Vidal, *op. cit.*, n. 72, p. 87; Chelodi, *op. cit.*, n. 13, p. 14; Gasparri, *op. cit.*, I, 152–153. Cappello adds that if Perrone, Liberatore and Taparelli knew of the existence of this document for certain, they would not have favored or followed the opinion which they did, denying competency to civil authority in the marriages of the unbaptized.

[51] Wernz-Vidal, *Ius Matrimoniale,* 87–88, *in nota.*

The Vicar-Apostolic of Western Tunking submitted this question: "An unbaptized man, who had entered marriage with an unbaptized woman, having omitted certain ceremonies, the omission of which is considered a diriment impediment to marriage according to the laws of Tunking, leaves this woman and takes as his second wife a Christian woman; he, now embracing the Christian religion, desires to receive Baptism. Is he held to make the interpellations of his first wife whom he deserted, as to whether or not she desires to become a Christian, and return to live with him, or at least cohabit with him peaceably and without contempt of God? If his first wife becomes a Christian, or at least agrees to live peaceably with him, is he bound to go back to her? If he becomes reconciled with his first wife and there is a true legitimate marriage between them, should they renew their matrimonial consent? To put it briefly, does a diriment impediment, established by an unbaptized legislator, or accepted through long-standing and common custom, render marriages void and invalid, if the marriages be contracted between unbaptized men and women?"

The reply of the Sacred Congregation, under the date of December 6, 1631, reads as follows: "Both the first and the second marriages are null; there is no need for the interpellations, but observing all things which should be observed, there may be a new marriage; and let there be given an instruction." [52]

[52] "Vir infidelis, qui cum muliere infideli matrimonium inierat, omissa quadam caeremonia, cuius omissio, iuxta Tunkinici regni leges regestas, censetur matrimonii impedimentum dirimens, ab ea muliere discessit et aliam uxorem christianam duxit; christianam ipse fidem amplectens, baptismum petit. Teneturne primam ab eo derelictam coniugem interpellare, an et ipsa Christi fidem profiteri et cum eo redire velit, an saltem pacifice cum eo et absque Creatoris contumelia cohabitare consentiat? Si christiana fieri aut saltem cum praefato viro pacifice cohabitare consentiat illa mulier, teneturne ad illam redire? Si cum priore hac coniuge, facta christiana, reconcilietur, et stet inter ambos verum et legitimum matrimonium, debetne ab iis renovari consensus? Uno verbo, impedimentum dirimens, a Principe infideli sancitum, aut apud gentem infidelem antiqua et communi invectum consuetudine, redditne irrita et invalida matrimonia inter viros et mulieres infideles cum tali impedimento contracta?"

Resp.: "Esse nullum primum et secundum matrimonium: non esse hic locum interpellationi, sed esse locum novum matrimonium, servatis servandis, et detur instructio."—*Collectanea S. C. P. F.*, n. 744.

The Instruction mentioned in the response was issued, and in September of the following year it was proposed for the approbation of the Cardinals who met in a Particular Congregation for China; though there is no mention that approbation was given by the Cardinals, Gasparri states that it probably was.[53] The Instruction sets up the general principle that marriages among the unbaptized are certainly under the legislative competency of civil rulers: ". . . Wherefore, although true marriage may exist among the unbaptized, it can only be considered under its natural and social aspect, and clearly, therefore, it is to be governed by the natural and civil law. From this it follows that civil rulers, whether Christian or pagan, possess a plenitude of power over the marriages of their unbaptized subjects; so that, by placing impediments which are not contrary to the natural or the divine law, they may impede not only the civil effects of such a marriage, but the marital bond itself. For there exists no reason whatsoever, why they, who by law can prescribe necessary solemnities and the form required for the legality and validity of other contracts, cannot do the same for the marriage contract of their unbaptized subjects; moreover, whatever is said concerning the statute law of civil rulers, may also be applied to legitimate custom which has received the force of law among unbaptized citizens." [54]

To this argument may also be added the one drawn from the common and constant practice of missionaries, who have always treated civil impediments and invalidating laws as affecting the

---

[53] Gasparri, *De Matrimonio,* I, n. 247, p. 152.

[54] ". . . Quare licet inter infideles verum sit matrimonium, tamen ad naturae et communitatis officium referri tantummodo potest, ac proinde a iure naturae ac civili plane est moderandum. Sequitur hinc Principes saeculares sive fideles sive infideles plenissimam potestatem retinere in matrimoniis subditorum infidelium; ut scilicet appositis impedimentis quae iuri naturali ac divino adversa non sint, eadem non solum quoad civiles effectus, sed etiam quoad coniugale vinculum penitus rescindant. Qui enim, ob Reipublicae bonum, suis legibus ad legitimitatem validitatemque ceterorum contractuum formam quamdam, et solemnitatibus praescribere possunt, cur id in matrimoniali infidelium subditorum contractu efficere nequeant, ratio non est; et quod de lege Principis saecularis hoc in casu dicitur, intellige etiam de legitima consuetudine, quae vim legis in subditos infideles adepta est."—*Collectanea S. C. P. F.*, n. 744, *not.* 1.

marriage bond among infidels, a practice which has received at least tacit approval of the Holy See.[55]

With the competency of civil authority thus established over the marriages of two infidels, it is apparent that two unbaptized persons could not validly enter a common law marriage whenever the statute law, or the unwritten law recognized by the jurisprudence of the State, forbids such marriages under pain of nullity. On the other hand, since a right at common law is considered to continue until it has been expressly abrogated, common law marriage among the unbaptized would be valid in any state if there be in that state neither statutes nor judicial interpretations requiring a form for the valid contracting of marriage.

ARTICLE 2. COMMON LAW MARRIAGE BETWEEN A BAPTIZED AND AN UNBAPTIZED PERSON

With the establishment of the competency of the Church's legislative power over marriages of the baptized, when they marry among themselves, and that of the state for marriages of the unbaptized among themselves, the question naturally arises: By what legislation is a common law marriage governed when contracted by one party who is baptized and one party who is not? Does each respective authority remain competent, the Church for the Christian, the state for the infidel, so that the requisites of both legislations must be fulfilled for the validity of a marriage entered by one subject from each jurisdiction or may one authority alone regulate the marriage?

The question of the legislative competency over such unions has arisen comparatively recently in the history of the Church. Prior to the 17th and 18th centuries, the impediment of disparity of cult, which forbade such unions, was rarely dispensed with. Nicolaus de Tudeschis, a Benedictine canonist of the 15th century (often called *Abbas Panormitanus* because he was the Archbishop of Palermo), enunciated as an almost absolute statement that there could be no marriage between a Christian and an infidel except when marriage had already been contracted prior to the con-

---

[55] Wernz-Vidal, *Ius Matrimoniale*, n. 73, p. 89; Cappello, *De Matrimonio*, n. 76, p. 92; Gasparri, *De Matrimonio*, I, n. 243, p. 149; Payen, *De Matrimonio*, I, n. 207, p. 154.

version of one of the parties.[56] Prior to the 16th century Reformation, the almost universal presence of Catholics throughout the civilized world precluded the necessity of the granting of this dispensation. In recent times, however, the applications for this dispensation have become numerous, and the question of the legislative control of the marriage of a baptized person with an infidel assumes a prominent place in matrimonial decisions.

There can be no doubt but that such unions are subject to the divine law, and therefore the supreme authority of the Church alone has the right to declare in what cases the divine law would forbid or annul such a marriage.[57]

So, too, the Church legislation remains competent by virtue of the fact that one of the parties to the marriage is, through Baptism, the Church's subject. "The same supreme authority (*of the Church*) has the exclusive right to constitute for baptized persons other impedient or diriment impediments of marriage, either by universal or particular law."[58] And for a baptized person entering any marriage, "The Holy See alone can attach to its prohibition (*of marriage*) the pain of nullity."[59] The freedom of the baptized party to such a marriage must be regulated and determined solely by the norms of Canon law.

Nor can there be any doubt but that a marriage between a Christian and an infidel would be null, if only one of the parties were bound by a diriment impediment. "Though the impediment may be on the part of only one of the parties, marriage is either illicit, or invalid, for both."[60] For the matrimonial contract, being a bilateral agreement, is indivisible, so that whatever *directly* affects one party to the contract *indirectly* affects the other. Thus the impediment of disparity of cult, which directly incapacitates the Catholic party, indirectly inhabilitates his unbap-

[56] "Inter fidelem et infidelem potest esse matrimonium, quod intellige quando matrimonium fuit contractum ante conversionem ad fidem. Alias inter dispares fidei non potest esse matrimonium."—Panormitanus (Nicolaus de Tudeschis), *Commentaria in Quinque Libros Decretalium* (5 vols. in 7, Venetiis, 1588), 1, IV, *de divortiis*, c. 8, n. 5.

[57] C. 1038, §1.

[58] C. 1038, §2.

[59] C. 1039, §2.

[60] C. 1036, §3; Payen, *De Matrimonio*, I, n. 200, p. 148.

tized, intended spouse. In this manner, infidels, who, according to canon 12, " are not held to laws which are purely Church laws," become indirectly bound by canonical prescriptions which legislate for marriage between a Christian and an unbaptized person. Those impediments which affect the relationship between the two parties to a marriage, and which would prevent this particular Christian from marrying this particular infidel, are called relative impediments.[61] An *absolute* impediment, on the contrary, is one which prevents a person from entering marriage with any other person whatsoever, irrespective of his condition, status, or relationship to the first party.[62]

The exclusiveness of the Church's competency in establishing matrimonial impediments for the baptized effectively precludes the establishment by the state of any *relative* impediment, which, though directly intended for the unbaptized party, would, nevertheless, indirectly bind the baptized party to the marriage. Any civil matrimonial impediment which even indirectly binds a Christian is a usurpation of the control over the marriages of Christians which Christ commissioned exclusively to the Church. Thus Pope Benedict XIV, in writing about a marriage between a Christian woman and a Jew, denied the competency of a law of the Emperor Theodosius which prohibited such a marriage. " This law," said the Pope, " inasmuch as it was established by a civil ruler, should have no force in marriage." [63]

Whether *absolute* impediments, decreed by the state and binding only the unbaptized party in a mixed marriage, would invalidate such unions, if the Catholic party were free, or dispensed from canonical impediments, is sharply controverted. For the present the question remains an open issue, since as yet there has been no official settlement of the question by the Holy See.

---

[61] " Impedimenta relativa sunt quibus una pars inhabilitatur, non absolute quidem, sed relate ad certas personas determinatis in adjunctis versantes."—Onclin, W., " De regimine Matrimonii Fidelem inter et Infidelem "—*Ephemerides Theologicae Lovanienses* (Lovanii: Universitas Catholica Lovanienses, 1924–), X (1933), 47–62, esp. 47. (Henceforth this work will be cited *ETL.*)

[62] Chelodi, *Jus Matrimoniale*, n. 35, p. 34.

[63] " Haec lex, utpote a laico principe condita, nullam habere vim in matrimoniis debet."—Benedictus XIV, ep. *Singulari*, 9 febr. 1749—*Fontes*, n. 349.

Many authors, including renowned canonists, maintain that an *absolute* civil diriment impediment binding only the infidel party would nullify his attempted marriage to a baptized person. Defending this opinion are Gasparri,[64] Vermeersch-Creuzen,[65] Vlaming,[66] Linneborn,[67] DeBecker,[68] Onclin,[69] Grentrup,[70] and Hilling.[71]

The opposite opinion, holding that civil law does not enter into consideration when an unbaptized person marries a baptized person, is maintained by Wernz,[72] Wernz-Vidal,[73] Cappello,[74] Chelodi,[75] DeSmet,[76] Payen,[77] Vromant,[78] Grandclaude [79] and Alford.[80]

The first of these two opinions, holding that the absolute, civil diriment opinion would nullify a mixed marriage, bases its argument on the competence of the state to legislate for its own subjects. Once this power of the state is admitted, " it follows," says

---

64 *De Matrimonio,* I, n. 256, pp. 160, 161.

65 *Epitome,* II, n. 278, p. 194.

66 *Praelectiones Iuris Matrimonii* (3 ed., 2 vols., Bussum in Hollandia, Vol. I, 1919, Vol. II, 1921), I, n. 195, pp. 167, 168.

67 *Grundriss des Eherechts nach dem Codex Iuris Canonici* (5 ed., Paderborn: Ferdinand Schöningh, 1933), 51, 52.

68 *De Matrimonio Praelectiones Canonicae* (2 ed., Louvain: Fr. Ceuterick, 1931), 25, 26.

69 " De regimine Matrimonii Fidelem inter et Infidelem."—*Ephemerides Theologicae Lovanienses,* X (1933), 47–62.

70 " Die Rassenmischehen in den deutschen Kolonien und das kanonische Recht."—*AKKR,* XCIV (1914), 1–34.

71 " Kanonistiches Gutachten über das Verbot der Rassenmischehen in den deutschen Kolonien."—*AKKR,* XCV (1915), 683–690.

72 *Ius Decretalium* (6 vols., Romae et Prati), Vol. IV, *Ius Matrimoniale* (1904), n. 60, p. 14.

73 *Ius Matrimoniale,* n. 52, pp. 65, 66.

74 *De Sacramentis,* III, pars. 1, n. 67, pp. 70, 71.

75 *Ius Matrimoniale,* n. 12, pp. 11, 12.

76 *De Sponsalibus et Matrimonio,* n. 438 *bis,* p. 380.

77 *De Matrimonio,* I, n. 203, p. 151.

78 *Jus Missionariorum,* Vol. V. *De Matrimonio* (Louvain: Museum Lessianum, 1931), pp. 5–9.

79 " Competence de l'État Touchant le Mariage des Infideles."—*Canoniste Contemporain, Le, X* (1887), 241–257; Grandclaude, *Ius Canonicum,* 3 vols., Parisiis (1883), III, 33.

80 *Jus Matrimoniale Comparatum,* n. 21, pp. 15, 16.

Gasparri,[81] "that the marriage in this case would be invalid because of canon 1036, §3, unless the civil authority had granted to its non-baptized subject a dispensation, which the Church cannot grant." The authors see no difficulty in the point that the marriage in question would fall under both jurisdictions as to the respective capability of the parties to enter the contract.

On the other hand, the second group of canonists argue that the competence of the state comes into conflict with the competence of the Church in this case. If the marriage in question presents such a conflict, as it seems to us to do, the rights of the Church should prevail. "For in any conflict between societies which are formally distinct," says Ottaviani, "the superior one, or that which has its end in a higher order should prevail, and to that society belongs the right to judge the extent and the solution of the conflict." [82]

That the two jurisdictions come into conflict may be readily seen by visualizing the different attitudes which the Church and the State would take towards a marriage entered into by Sempronia, a baptized Catholic, and Titius, unbaptized, who marry with the proper dispensation from disparity of cult, but with Titius disclosing that he was under a civil impediment of age which prohibited his valid marriage. Such an impediment, according to Vlaming, "binds the unbaptized person directly, or by reason of his subjection (*to the State*); indirectly, however, or by reason of his connection (*with the unbaptized*) it binds the faithful party." [83] According to the Church Sempronia would be free and capable to enter this marriage, since her freedom to marry, like her inability to marry, must be determined by the

[81] *De Matrimonio,* I, n. 256, pp. 160, 161.

[82] "In conflictu inter societates formaliter distinctas, superior, seu quae finem altioris ordinis habet, praevalere debet, eidemque competit iudicium ferre de ipsius conflictus terminis et solutione."—Ottaviani, *Institutiones Iuris Publici Ecclesiastici,* I, n. 82, p. 162.

[83] ". . . impedimentum civile tali casu tenere, directe quidem, seu ratione subjectionis, partem infidelem; indirecte vero, seu ratione connexionis, partem infidelem."—Vlaming, *Praelectiones Juris Matrimonii,* 168; Onclin ("De regimine Matrimonii Fidelem inter et Infidelem."—*ETL,* X [1933], 57) denies that any conflict arises as to freedom to marry, since he claims nothing militates against a twofold competency, i.e., of the Church and State, in this question.

norms of Canon Law. Only the Church can establish an impediment for her;[84] only the freedom from Church impediments determines her ability to marry. In this case the Church determines Sempronia is free, according to canonical norms. Yet Vlaming (and his arguments are consonant with the others who agree with him) maintains that Sempronia is not free to enter this marriage, and precisely because the civil impediment which directly affects Titius indirectly binds her. The State maintains that Sempronia is not free to enter this marriage; the Church having canonically evaluated her status maintains that she is free. In such a conflict the jurisdiction of the Church, as being that of a higher society, should prevail.

Vlaming and his colleagues admit a canonical impediment would deter Sempronia from marrying. Logically, her freedom must be admitted if no canonical impediments are discovered.

The arguments which deny a state the right to legislate a relative impediment rest on the grounds that the state cannot even indirectly bind a baptized person by matrimonial impediments. For this reason, the impediment of disparity of cult, legislated by Theodosius, was declared null.[85] The same arguments hold true when an absolute impediment is considered in relation to a specific marriage. Though in the abstract a relative impediment affects only one party, yet in the concrete, when a particular marriage is considered, the absolute inability of one party to marry becomes so specified that indirectly it affects the other party to the marriage. The connection of the two parties, which, according to Vlaming,[86] extends the effect of the absolute civil impediment so that it indirectly affects the baptized person, must rather so relate the two parties, that the Church's jurisdiction, which in the abstract is not competent over the infidel, now is competent, by virtue of the connection of the two parties. This principle of the connection of the unbaptized person to the baptized person is universally recognized in the judicial forum of the Church; it is equally valid in the legislative realm.[87]

---

[84] C. 1038, §2.

[85] *Supra*, p. 78.

[86] *Loc. cit.*

[87] C. 1567; Wernz-Vidal, *Ius Matrimoniale*, n. 52, p. 66.

The practice of the Church, in conceding dispensations from disparity of cult without taking care to see to the freedom of the unbaptized person from civil impediments, confirms this argument.[88]

Finally, as Vromant points out,[89] this opinion is confirmed by the application of canon 1127, in which case, as he says, "it is stated that it is in favor of the Catholic party, and sometimes, it seems, to the detriment of the infidel, that 'in a doubtful matter the privilege of the faith enjoys the favor of law.'" The contrary opinion, which forbids a marriage under pain of nullity, would deny the Catholic or baptized party the privilege of marrying an infidel who is of age according to the natural and Canon law, yet under age according to the civil law.

Nor has the Church declared that the infidel in this case is held by the absolute impediments of Canon law. It is held that the Church could do so if she wished,[90] but that she has not actually so legislated.[91]

In summary, then, a common law marriage in which at least one of the parties is baptized, even though not a Catholic, must be governed not by civil laws, which might prohibit common law marriages under pain of nullity, but by the Canon law of the Church. Such a marriage would easily be possible for a baptized non-Catholic and an unbaptized person, since by the Baptism of one party the marriage comes under the competency of the Church legislation; by virtue of the non-Catholicity of the baptized party, he would not be held to the canonical form of marriage, and unless baptized in the Catholic Church, by the impediment of disparity of cult; and despite the neglect of any

---

[88] Payen, *De Matrimonio,* I, n. 202, p. 151; Vromant, *Ius Missionariorum,* V (*De Matrimonio*), n. 7, p. 8. The Holy Office on Sept. 20, 1854, in speaking about a marriage of two infidels, invalidly contracted because of a civil impediment, declared that if either party were converted, their consent was to be renewed after a dispensation was obtained from ecclesiastical impediments; but no mention was made about the impediments decreed by civil law.—*Collectanea S. C. P. F.*, I, n. 1104.

[89] *Loc. cit.*

[90] DeSmet, *De Sponsalibus et Matrimonio,* n. 547, p. 477.

[91] DeSmet, *loco citato;* Cappello, *De Sacramentis,* III, pars 1, n. 336, p. 432.

formalities of the civil law and despite any civil impediment, v. g. of age, which might affect the unbaptized party, the marriage would be valid provided no impediment of the natural law hindered either party and no impediment of the Church law hindered the baptized party.

CHAPTER VII

Procedures Possible in Invalid Common Law Marriages

Once a common law marriage has been discovered to be null, there are, theoretically at least, four possible means of procedure:[1]

1. The marriage may be validated, if the parties are willing and if no impediment stands in the way;

2. The marriage may be declared null, and the parties made to separate if they have not already done so.

(Either of these two methods must be followed if the nullity of the marriage is known, either to the parties or to others; otherwise, formal sin by the parties, or scandal to others would result.[2])

3. If the nullity of the marriage be known to either party, or to both parties, but not to others, and if the cause of the nullity cannot be removed, it might be permitted, in rare instances, that the man and woman be allowed to live together as brother and sister.

4. If the nullity of the marriage be unknown to both parties and to others, and if the cause of the nullity cannot be removed, then the parties may be left in good faith as often more serious consequences would follow the disclosure of the nullity of their marriage.

---

[1] Wernz-Vidal, *Ius Matrimoniale,* n. 651, pp. 787, 788; Payen, *De Matrimonio,* II, n. 2518, pp. 849, 850; DeSmet, *De Sponsalibus et Matrimonio,* n. 720, p. 615.

[2] If the parties cannot be immediately separated, because, for example, the man is seriously ill and requires the ministrations of the woman, the couple should declare before witnesses that they are ready and willing either to validate the marriage, or to separate as soon as possible; in the meantime they must avoid every occasion of sin by following the precautions suggested by the pastor. Cf. DeSmet, *op. cit.,* n. 721, p. 616.

These last two methods of procedure, it must be insisted, may be followed only when the nullity of the marriage is occult, namely, it is not at present known to others, and it is prudently foreseen that it will not become divulged in the future.[3] Otherwise, grave scandal would result if the unmarried parties were allowed to continue to cohabit.

These four remedies will be discussed with reference to the advisability of using each.

A. Validation of a Common Law Marriage

When the only reason for the nullity of a common law marriage is the lack of the formalities required in the valid contracting of marriage, the union may be validated merely by the contracting of marriage in the prescribed form.[4] If a Catholic were involved, this would mean the renewal of consent in the presence of the pastor, the Ordinary, or duly delegated priest, and two witnesses.[5] The new celebration of the marriage may be secret, according to Wernz-Vidal, if the nullity of the marriage were occult.[6] The secret celebration does not mean the omission of the required witnesses, but rather the celebration of the marriage before witnesses who are friends of the bridal couple, and the avoidance of publicity, which would in this case be most embarrassing.[7] If the nullity of the marriage were publicly known, then the celebration of the marriage must be public so that all scandal attending the sinful cohabitation may be removed; however, DeSmet suggests that the celebration may be carried out secretly, i.e., before the pastor and friendly witnesses, if the Bishop were to allow it and if he would see to it that, by the publication of the fact of the celebration of the marriage, scandal would be allayed.[8]

If one of the parties to a null common law marriage should refuse to validate the union by observing the proper formalities,

---

[3] Cf. c. 2197, §3.

[4] C. 1137.

[5] C. 1094.

[6] *Ius Matrimoniale,* n. 655, p. 791.

[7] DeSmet, *De Sponsalibus et Matrimonio,* n. 729, p. 620.

[8] *Loc. cit.*

then, provided the consent of both parties still endures, a dispensation from the law requiring the form of marriage might be granted, or a *sanatio in radice* might be issued. Either would obviate the necessity of contracting a formal marriage. Neither could be granted if scandal were to result from its use, because, namely, the nullity of the marriage was known, while the validation of it would remain secret. The *sanatio in radice,* besides being a dispensation from the form of marriage, contains also a retroactive effect so that the marriage would, in the eyes of the law, be considered valid from its beginning, i.e., from the moment when the parties first exchanged matrimonial consent.[9] A *sanatio* could not be granted except when a naturally valid consent, once given, continues to exist; and even though true consent were lacking in the beginning of the common law marriage, but later given, the *sanatio* may be granted so that the marriage will be considered valid from the time the consent was given.[10]

B. *Declaration of Nullity of a Common Law Marriage*

If the marriage is null, a declaration of nullity should be obtained, especially in the following cases:

1. If it is impossible to validate the marriage;
2. If the parties are unwilling to live together as man and wife;
3. If the danger of perversion for one of the parties, or some other grave reason should indicate the necessity of a new marriage for one of the parties.[11]

In speaking of the declaration of nullity of a common law marriage, we shall prescind from the possible presence of some impediment (which may as easily be present in this type of marriage as in a formal marriage), since an impediment in a common law marriage would have no special effect, nor require special treatment, because of the common law nature of the marriage. The nullity of the marriage as treated here will signify the nullity which might arise precisely because no formal ceremonies or rites were observed in entering the union. If, together with this lack

---

[9] C. 1138—Ayrinhac-Lydon, *Marriage Legislation in the New Code of Canon Law* (revised ed., New York: Benziger Brothers, 1932), 342–346.

[10] Cc. 1139, 1140.

[11] Chelodi, *Ius Matrimoniale,* n. 163, p. 203.

of form, an impediment should co-exist, that impediment must be carefully considered and treated as the nature of it may demand.

The declaration of nullity of a common law marriage may be given without the formalities of judicial procedure, or it may be issued at the conclusion of a solemn trial.

The declaration of nullity, without the formalities of judicial procedure, may be issued by the Ordinary, or by the pastor after consulting his Ordinary, as often as the nullity is clearly established in the preliminary investigation prior to a marriage.[12] This declaration may be issued as often as anyone bound to enter the formal marriage prescribed by the Code, fails to do so. Thus the *1936 Instruction*[13] states: "If anyone was certainly bound to the canonical form of the celebration of marriage and contracted marriage only civilly or if he entered the marriage in the presence of a non-Catholic minister, or if apostates from the Catholic faith were married civilly in apostasy or in some alien rite, neither judicial solemnities nor the intervention of the *Defensor Vinculi* are required to ascertain the freedom of such to marry. Such cases can be settled by the Ordinary himself, or by the pastor after consulting the Ordinary in the investigation preceding marriage, as indicated in canon 1019 and subsequent canons. However, if a doubt should remain about the conditions stated in paragraph one of the present article, the question is to be decided according to the ordinary procedure of the law."[14] The "doubt" mentioned refers to any doubt as to "whether the existence of an impediment or cause of nullity is clearly established by a certain and authentic document which is beyond contradiction or exception."[15]

The pastor then, after consulting the Ordinary, or the Ordinary

---

[12] *PCI,* 16 oct. 1919—*AAS,* XI (1919), 479; Bouscaren, *Canon Law Digest,* I, 810, 811.

[13] The term *1936 Instruction* will be used to indicate the "Instructio servanda a tribunalibus diocesanis in pertractandis causis de nullitate matrimoniorum," issued by the Sacred Congregation of Sacraments Aug. 15, 1936, and published in the *AAS,* XXVIII (1936), 312–370.

[14] *1936 Instruction,* art. 231—*AAS,* XXVIII (1936), 313; Doheny, *Canonical Procedure in Matrimonial Cases,* 377.

[15] *1936 Instruction,* art. 228—*loc. cit.*

himself can declare a marriage null only when the following conditions are verified:

1. It must be established for certain that at least one of the parties was bound to observe the canonical form of marriage. This fact could be established by a certain and authentic document if: (a) Records were adduced to show that the party was born of Catholic parents and baptized in the Catholic Church; or (b) the party was born of non-Catholic parents,[16] but was baptized in the Catholic Church, and raised as a Catholic; or (c) was converted to the Catholic Church from heresy or schism.[17]

2. It must be established for certain that the canonical form was omitted, or at least that no dispensation from the form or no *sanatio in radice* had been obtained. Proof of non-observance of the Catholic form of marriage may be secured by a search of the records of the parishes in which it was possible for the couple to have been married. The wisdom of the provision of the *1936 Instruction,*[18] requiring the pastor to consult the Ordinary before he declares a marriage null on the grounds of defective form, becomes apparent when it is remembered that certainty concerning the absence of the canonical contracting of marriage cannot be established, unless a search of the diocesan records shows that no validation has taken place, perhaps in another parish or diocese, and that no dispensation from the form of marriage and no *sanatio in radice* has been granted.

This recourse to the Ordinary is so strongly insisted upon that the Ordinary is not allowed to decree by general mandate that the pastors obtain a sworn statement concerning the freedom of the parties about to marry, thus obviating the necessity of recourse to the Ordinary.[19]

---

[16] Non-Catholic parents include those of whom only one is a non-Catholic, or an apostate. Cf. *PCI,* 20 iulii 1929, II—*AAS,* XXI (1929), 573; Bouscaren, *Canon Law Digest,* 543; also *PCI,* 17 feb. 1930—*AAS,* XXII (1930), 195; Bouscaren, *op. cit.,* 544.

[17] Cf. canon 1099, §1, which also states that these persons are bound to the Catholic form of marriage even though they may have later apostatized from the true faith.

[18] Art. 231.

[19] This practice was forbidden by a decree of the Sacred Congregation of the Sacraments given on Feb. 6, 1920 for the Diocese of Mainz; this decree is found in *AKKR,* C (1920), 28 sqq.

Furthermore, no matter what the cause of nullity of a marriage may be, the Code forbids the remarriage of a Catholic before there is legal proof of the invalidity of that marriage.[20] This legal proof must be established either through the formal procedure of a canonical trial or through the informal procedure outlined in the *1936 Instruction,* art. 226, sqq.[21] Therefore when the Ordinary is consulted according to the provision of article 231 of the *1936 Instruction* he may forbid the pastor to allow a new marriage until some authentic document be issued by himself legally attesting to the nullity of the null marriage. If this be the case, it seems the pastor may under no circumstances proceed to a new marriage after merely *consulting* the Ordinary, but rather he must await in such cases the judgment of the Ordinary.

Diocesan statutes many times state what documents must be submitted before a declaration of nullity according to the informal procedure will be granted. Usually the pastor or priest submitting the case to the Ordinary is required to furnish a marriage certificate showing that the parties were married and that there exists cause for proceeding to declare the marriage null.[22] Since in a common law marriage it will usually be impossible to adduce any certificate of marriage, it is suggested that as a substitute a sworn statement signed by trustworthy witnesses be adduced to show that the parties lived together and were known as man and wife. This testimony of cohabitation and repute of marriage will give rise at least to a presumed or putative marriage; such a marriage may then form the basis for the declaration of nullity which is sought.

In the informal procedure for declaring a marriage null because of defective form, as outlined in article 231 of the *1936 Instruction,*[23] it will suffice to show that at least one of the parties was held to observe the canonical form of marriage, and despite

---

[20] C. 1069, §2.

[21] Instr. S. C. Sacr., 29 iun. 1941—*AAS,* XXII (1941), 539 sqq; *The Jurist* (Washington, D. C.: The School of Canon Law, The Catholic University of America, 1941-), II, No. 1 (Jan. 1942), Supplement.

[22] Such a marriage record is, for example, required in the Diocese of Fargo. Cf. n. 799 of the Fargo Synod—*Synodus Diocesana Fargensis Prima* (Milwauchiae: Ex typographia Bruce, 1941), p. 165.

[23] *AAS,* XXVIII (1936), 313.

this obligation, failed to do so; the marriage may then be declared canonically null and void. Because civil laws may recognize the common law marriage as valid, some authors counsel that the parties be advised to procure a civil decree of divorce or dissolution before allowing a second marriage.[24]

Since the informal procedure of article 231 of the *1936 Instruction* is not a judicial trial, it is not necessary that anyone act as plaintiff, but merely that the facts be submitted to the judgment of the Ordinary. Therefore the facts may be submitted and a petition for a declaration of nullity may be made by a non-Catholic, despite the fact that in matrimonial causes, i.e., formally tried marriage cases, a non-Catholic, baptized or unbaptized, may not act as plaintiff.[25]

A non-Catholic petitioner, who requested from the Holy Office a declaration of nullity from his marriage because of the impediment of disparity of cult, received the reply: "The case may be treated by the Ordinary according to the norms of can. 1990–1992." [26] While a defective form case is not included in the prescriptions of canons 1990–1992, the procedure for a defective form case is very similar to that of the cases therein treated, as is. apparent from a reading of articles 226–231 of the *1936 Instruction.* The word "impediment" in canons 1990–1992 must receive strict interpretation and their use may not be invoked unless the impediment which forms the basis for attack is specifically mentioned in these Canons.[27]

---

[24] Ayrinhac-Lydon, *Marriage Legislation in the New Code of Canon Law,* n. 327, p. 365.

[25] S. C. S. O., 27 ian. 1928—*AAS,* XX (1928), 75; Bouscaren, *Canon Law Digest,* I, 762, 763.

[26] C. S. C. O., 20 apr. 1931, (Private)—Bouscaren, *Canon Law Digest,* II, 267, 268; *Jus Pontificium,* LIX (1932), 134; Chelodi, *Jus Matrimoniale,* n. 180, p. 224.

[27] As the Apostolic Delegate to the United States has pointed out: "The language employed by canon 1990 and article 226 of the Instruction must be understood and applied exactly in the literal sense without any amplifications or extensive interpretations whatsoever."—Letter of Apostolic Delegate on Handling of Marriage Cases in the United States (Apostolic Delegation, U. S., 23 Sept., 1938), Private—Bouscaren, *Canon Law Digest,* Suppl. p. 194.

However, as will be mentioned later, the lack of form does come under

If a common law marriage is not certainly null, recourse must be had to the ordinary course of procedure, namely, that of a formal, judicial trial, in order to declare the marriage null.[28] Insistence on this point was emphasized by the Apostolic Delegate to the United States in his letter of 1938 to the Ordinaries of this country:

" In handling cases involving the total lack of the juridical form of marriage, as envisaged in article 231 of the Instruction of August 15, 1936, the complete ruling of the second paragraph of the same article must always be strictly observed, namely: '*Si quod dubium supersit de recensitis conditionibus in §1, quaestio ordinarii processus tramite definienda est.*' The Sacred Congregation expressly and solemnly charges all Ordinaries *graviter onerata eorum conscientia* to exercise the most unremitting vigilance over such cases, since any abuse in these matters could seriously jeopardize the sanctity of the marriage bond, as well as the dignity of ecclesiastical tribunals." [29]

C. *Fraternal Cohabitation*

The permission for a man and woman who are not, and who, because of some impediment, cannot lawfully become man and wife, to live together is rarely granted and then only for most serious reasons. This remedy, or solution for invalid marriages, is not mentioned in the law of the Church. However, it is mentioned by canonists, who maintain that it is theoretically possible, though because it is most dangerous, in practice, rarely admitted.[30] The danger in tolerating this situation is self-evident: A person is obliged not only to avoid sin, but also to avoid the occasion of sin, namely, any external circumstance which, because

---

the term impediment when, in reference to c. 1971, " impediment " includes also " the impediments improperly so-called," namely those listed in c. 1089–1103. Cf. *PCI*, 12 mart. 1929—*AAS*, XXI (1929), 171; Bouscaren, *Canon Law Digest*, I, 807.

[28] *1936 Instruction*, art. 231, §2—*AAS*, XXVIII (1936), 313; Bouscaren, *Canon Law Digest*, II, 259.

[29] Bouscaren, *Canon Law Digest*, Suppl., 194.

[30] Cappello, *De Sacramentis*, III, pars 2, n. 841, p. 372; Wernz-Vidal, *Jus Matrimoniale*, n. 651, p. 788; DeSmet, *De Sponsalibus et Matrimonio*, nn. 722, 723, pp. 616, 617; Chelodi, *Jus Matrimoniale*, n. 163, p. 203.

of the nature of the circumstance or because of the human frailty of a person in such a circumstance, would cause or induce a person to sin.[31] Ordinarily, but not necessarily, the cohabitation of an unmarried couple would be construed as an occasion of sin for the parties. Yet because it is possible, under certain circumstances and by the exercise of prudence and precaution, for a man and woman to live together without sin, this condition may be permitted as a solution of the problem of a null common law marriage. The following conditions, however, must be verified:

1. It must be the only solution to the problem.[32] Thus it must be impossible, because of some impediment, for the parties to have their marriage validated. It must also be impossible for the parties to separate, e.g., an aged couple live together; the man is seriously ill, and the woman's care is needed, since no other means are available to provide for the infirm man.

2. The nullity of the marriage must be unknown to others.[33] This remedy may never be used, when because the marriage was publicly known to be null, scandal would arise if the parties were not made to separate. As Payen points out,[34] fraternal cohabitation may be permitted when a marriage commonly thought to be valid is known to the parties to be null because of the certain, antecedent and perpetual impotency of the man.

3. Proper precautionary measures must be taken to forestall the danger of incontinence in the parties. Separate sleeping quarters must be used[35] and whatever precautionary measures may be suggested by the pastor or the Ordinary should be followed. Since the declaration of nullity cannot be made unless the Ordinary is consulted, it seems proper that the granting of this decision should be done only by the pastor, after consulting the Ordinary, if not by the Ordinary himself.

D. *Dissimulation*

The disclosure to the parties of the nullity of a marriage may,

---

31 Sabetti-Barrett, *Compendium Theologiae Moralis*, n. 800, p. 781.

32 Wernz-Vidal, *loc. cit.*

33 DeSmet, *De Sponsalibus et Matrimonio*, n. 722, p. 616.

34 *De Matrimonio*, II, n. 2524, p. 852.

35 DeSmet, *op. cit.*, n. 724, p. 617.

in some instances, effect more harm than good. When the parties would refuse to break off a cohabitation which, because of some impediment, could not become a valid marriage, and when the parties at present believe their union to be a valid marriage, any enlightenment as to their true status would mean that whereas they now commit material sins, in the future they would be committing formal sins.[36] If the nullity of a marriage were entirely unknown, except to the priest who discovers it, he may, under the circumstances just described, keep secret the fact of nullity, thus leaving the good faith of the parties undisturbed. This procedure is called dissimulation. If a priest leaves the parties in good faith, he must make certain that their good faith is not disturbed by any action of his, and he must likewise from time to time make sure that their good faith perseveres. If their good faith ceases, even in only one of the parties, or if the true nature of the union should ever become known to someone else, the priest may no longer remain silent, but should inform the parties about the nullity of their marriage.[37]

---

[36] A material sin is committed when a law is involuntarily broken; a formal sin is had when a law, binding in conscience, is knowingly and willingly broken. Cf. Sabetti-Barrett, *Compendium Theologiae Moralis*, n. 125, p. 127.

[37] DeSmet, *De Sponsalibus et Matrimonio*, n. 724, p. 617.

CHAPTER VIII

Proof of Common Law Marriage

ARTICLE 1. COMPETENT JUDICIAL POWER OVER COMMON LAW MARRIAGES

Though the mutual consent of the contracting parties effects a common law marriage, their mutual consent is powerless to dissolve or modify the marital contract. For marriage, by its divine institution, is indissoluble, and despite whatever contrary practices were permitted under the law of the Old Testament, Jesus Christ recalled and restored marriage to its pristine nature of an indissoluble, monogamous union. As Pope Pius XI proclaimed: ". . . let it be repeated as an immutable and inviolable fundamental doctrine that matrimony was not instituted or restored by man but by God; not by man were the laws made to strengthen and confirm and elevate it but by God, the Author of nature, and by Christ our Lord by whom nature was redeemed, and hence these laws cannot be subject to any human decrees or to any contrary pact even of the spouses themselves."[1] Even in civil legislation, the inability of the parties to proclaim their own dissolution of a marriage is recognized. A publication by the United States Government declares: "The element of contract is important at the inception of marriage in establishing the relation. When once established however, this relation is a matter of public concern, and the parties cannot terminate, dissolve, or modify their contract by any subsequent agreement. The rights

---

[1] Pius XI, ep. encycl. "*Casti connubii*," 31 dec. 1930—*AAS*, XXII (1930), 539; English translation from *Five Great Encyclicals* (New York: The Paulist Press, 1939), 78.

and obligations arising out of the relation are fixed by law." [2]

Canon 1960 asserts that "Matrimonial cases between baptized persons belong by proper and exclusive right to the ecclesiastical judge." This principle is repeated in the Instruction, issued in 1936 by the Sacred Congregation of Sacraments, for the purpose of regulating the actions of diocesan tribunals in handling marriage cases; and to remove any ambiguity which might result from the wording of canon 1016, the following is significantly added in the Instruction: "This holds true even if only one party is baptized." [3]

For Baptism removes a person from the jurisdiction of civil courts, in sacred matters, just as it does from the legislative power of the State in these affairs.[4] Even though only one party

---

[2] Dep't. of Commerce and Labor, Bureau of the Census, *Marriage and Divorce*, I, 182, 183. The outlook of English law on this point is similar, as expressed in the words of Lord Robertson, reprinted on the same page of the publication just mentioned:

"Marriage is a contract *sui generis*, and differing in some respects from all other contracts, so that the rules of law which are applicable in expounding and enforcing other contracts may not apply to this. The contract of marriage is the most important of all human transactions. It is the very basis of the whole fabric of civilized society. The status of marriage is *juris gentium*, and the foundation of it, like that of all other contracts, rests on the consent of the parties; but it differs from other contracts in this, that the rights, obligations, or duties arising from it are not left entirely to be regulated by the agreements of the parties, but are, to a certain extent, matters of municipal regulation over which the parties have no control by any declaration of their will; it confers the status of legitimacy on children, with all the consequential rights, duties and privileges thence arising; gives rise to the relations of consanguinity and affinity; in short, it pervades the whole system of civilized society. Unlike other contracts, it cannot in general, amongst civilized nations, be dissolved by mutual consent, and it subsists in full force, even although one of the parties should be forever rendered incapable, as in the case of incurable insanity, or the like, from performing his part of the mutual contract. No wonder that the rights, duties, and obligations arising from so important a contract should not be left to the discretion or caprice of the contracting parties, but should be regulated in many important particulars by the laws of every civilized country."

[3] *1936 Instruction*, art. 1—*AAS*, XXVIII (1936), 314; Doheny, *Canonical Procedure in Matrimonial Cases*, 8.

[4] C. 87.

to a common law marriage were baptized, that marriage would be adjudicated by the ecclesiastical tribunal, as often as there arose a question concerning the marriage itself, or those things inseparably connected with the marriage bond. Thus, inseparably connected with the marriage bond would be the question of the freedom of the parties to contract marriage, questions concerning the existence, the worth, the canonical effects and the dissolution of formal betrothals (though these would seldom occur prior to a common law marriage); likewise, all questions of the existence, the validity, the canonical effects, v. gr. legitimacy, the convalidation and the dissolution of the marriage itself, and finally any question pertaining to the dissolution of conjugal life, i.e., separation as to bed, board, and mutual cohabitation.[5] If, in a case brought to trial concerning any of these matters, at least one of the parties concerned, whether plaintiff or defendant, were validly baptized, the ecclesiastical judge alone would be competent.[6]

Because at times, the merely civil effects, such as the distribution of property, or the payment of civil taxes, may form the object of a trial, the Church declares: "Cases involving the merely civil effects of marriage belong to the civil court, according to the regulations of canon 1016, if they are introduced as principal actions. However, if they are merely incidental and accessory to a case, they can be judged by the ecclesiastical judge in virtue of his proper authority."[7] Thus, when only the property rights of the parties to a common law marriage are involved, the State can and should decide the question. If during an ecclesiastical trial concerning the validity of a common law marriage, the question of property settlement must be decided, the ecclesiastical judge is competent and may decide the question, though as Wernz-Vidal suggests, it would be more expedient to remand the case of property settlement to the civil courts.[8]

Since, as has been stated, the will of the parties is ineffectual to modify or abrogate the obligations of marriage, the Church declares: "Marriage cases involving the matrimonial bond cannot

[5] Cappello, *De Sacramentis,* III, pars I, n. 60, p. 63.

[6] *1936 Instruction,* art. I, §3.

[7] *1936 Instruction,* art. I, §2; c. 1961.

[8] *Ius Matrimoniale,* n. 687, p. 827.

be settled by any private agreement of the parties or consorts, or by compromise through arbitration, or by a decisory oath; but only by public authority in virtue of a sentence of a competent tribunal or of an Ordinary in the summary cases mentioned in c. 1990."[9]

Thus far, it has been stated that the Church enjoys judicial competency over those marriages in which at least one of the parties is baptized. This competency remains the same whether the Baptism of one of the parties precedes the marriage, or whether after marriage, one of the two infidels to the marriage becomes a Christian.[10]

Over the marriage of two unbaptized persons the Church ordinarily exercises no competency, since such unions, entered by two people who are outside of her pale, are not of concern to the Church. It might happen, however, that an unbaptized person, who had entered a common law marriage with another infidel, has deserted that union, and now desires to marry a Catholic. In such circumstances, the Church could not determine whether the Catholic party were free to marry, until the marriage of the other party had been investigated and its validity or nullity established. In such a case, the determination of the freedom to marry of the Catholic party belongs to the Church. Specifically, "the pastor whom the law entitles to assist at the marriage shall in good time inquire whether there is any impediment to the marriage,"[11] since "before marriage is contracted it must be certain that there are no obstacles to its valid and licit celebration."[12] The pastor of the Catholic, learning about the existence of a previous common law marriage on the part of the infidel, must seek the aid of his Ordinary, who by virtue of the connection of the cases, becomes competent even over the marriage of two infidels. As Wernz-Vidal states: "Because of the connection of cases in mixed marriages, which have been or are about to be contracted, it can easily happen, that a decision must be made concerning another marriage contracted in infidelity, and perhaps, dissolved by

[9] *1936 Instruction,* art. 1, §3; Cf. cc. 1834; 1835; 1927, §1; 1930.

[10] Payen, *De Matrimonio,* III, n. 2650, p. 518.

[11] C. 1020, §1.

[12] C. 1019, §1.

divorce. In these cases, because of the faithful party, the sole competent judge is the ecclesiastical judge, for it is up to him to decide concerning the freedom to marry of the faithful party. This judgment he cannot render, unless it be first settled concerning the validity or nullity of the marriage contracted, or deserted in infidelity. If these cases, because of their difficulty, be not referred in the first instance to the Holy See at once, they should, it seems, be decided by the Bishop of the place wherein the Catholic party has his domicile, according to the decree of the S. C. Inq. of June 30, 1892, and June 23, 1903, which agree with C. 1964." [13]

The decrees of the Sacred Congregation of the Roman and universal Inquisition, to which references are made in this quotation, concern the procedure to be followed when only one of the parties to a marriage is a Catholic, and state that the proper Ordinary is to be determined by the place of domicile of the Catholic; thus they agree with canon 1964 which states: ". . . In all other (*i.e., than those reserved to the Holy Father or the Holy See*) matrimonial cases the judge competent to try the case is the judge of the place or diocese in which the marriage was contracted, or in which the defendant—or, if one of the married parties is a non-Catholic, the place in which the Catholic—has a domicile or quasi-domicile." [14]

In 1925 the following question was submitted to the Holy Office by the Archbishop of Friburg: "Whether an ecclesiastical

---

[13] "Praeterea propter connexionem causarum in hisce matrimoniis mixtis contractis vel contrahendis facile fieri potest, ut iudicium quoque sit ferendum de alio matrimonio antea in infidelitate celebrato, imo forte per divortium separato. Quibus in causis pariter ratione *patris fidelis* solus competens est judex ecclesiasticus; nam ad ipsum spectat iudicare de *status libertate* eiusdem fidelis. Quod iudicium dari nequit, nisi praevie constet de valore vel nullitate alicuius matrimonii in infidelitate contracti vel separati. Quae causae si propter difficultatem in prima instantia non statim ad Sedem Apostolicam deferantur, ex paritate decreta S. C. Inq., 30 iun. 1892, et 23 iun. 1903, quibus consonant can. 1964, coram Episcopo *domicilii partis catholicae* videntur esse definiendae."—Wernz-Vidal, *Jus Matrimoniale,* n. 687, p. 827, *in nota.*

[14] S. C. S. Off., 30 iun. 1892—*ASS,* XXVI (1893-1894), 753; *Fontes,* n. 1157; S. C. Inq., 23 iun. 1903—*ASS,* XXXVI (1903-1904), 165-166; *Fontes,* n. 1265.

tribunal can pass on the validity of a marriage between two non-Catholics, at the instance of the non-Catholic party who now wishes to marry a Catholic, or at the instance of the Catholic party who is about to marry a non-Catholic, or at the instance of the Promoter of Justice alone?" The reply to the Archbishop, which was never published in the *Acta Apostolicae Sedis,* was: "Recourse is to be had in each case." [15] Though this reply, which is a private one to the Archbishop of Friburg, is not binding on the universal Church, it may serve, nevertheless, as a helpful directive norm for any diocesan tribunal which encounters a similar case.

The ecclesiastical judge who presides over the case of two infidels applies, as Kay points out, not only the divine natural law and the divine positive law, but also the civil law in force in the place and at the time of the contracting of the marriage.[16]

ARTICLE 2. THE RIGHT TO IMPUGN A COMMON LAW MARRIAGE

Before a formal trial to determine the nullity of a marriage may be started, some person, having the right in law to do so, must institute proceedings, either by accusing the marriage or by denouncing it as invalid. For "the Church cannot take cognizance of or decide any matrimonial case unless a regular accusation or a legal petition has been presented." [17]

To "impugn a marriage" means to institute an action before the competent tribunal for the purpose either of impeding a future marriage, or of declaring null a marriage already contracted, or of obtaining a separation of the married couple as to bed and board.[18] The term "impugn" will be used in the second of these senses, namely, to institute an action with a view towards obtaining a declaration of nullity. In speaking of common law marriage the grounds for impugning or denouncing the marriage will

---

[15] This reply of the Holy Office, given April 8, 1925, was first reported in *Periodica,* XIV (1925), 166, and is translated into English by Bouscaren, *Canon Law Digest,* I, 763.

[16] Kay, *Competence in Matrimonial Procedure,* The Catholic University of America Canon Law Studies, n. 53 (Washington, D. C.: The Catholic University of America, 1929), 39.

[17] C. 1970; *1936 Instruction,* art. 34—*AAS,* XXVIII (1936), 313.

[18] Coronata, *Institutiones Iuris Canonici,* III, n. 1485, p. 422.

be precisely the lack of canonical form, prescinding from the possible presence of other impediments which might also be present. Lack of form is the distinctive, characteristic feature of common law marriages.

The right to impugn a marriage is limited so that none but the parties to the marriage and the Promoter of Justice, and these only under certain circumstances, may legally impugn the bond of a marriage.[19] Even the Ordinary should not impugn the marriage, when it is brought to his attention that a certain couple may be living in an invalid marriage. He should refer the case to the Promoter of Justice, who, in turn, should impugn the marriage, as the law requires or permits.[20] Under the law prior to the Code, anyone of the faithful could impugn a marriage, which was invalid because of a public impediment.[21] The law of the Code, however, and of the *1936 Instruction,* excludes all other persons except the parties to the marriage and the Promoter of Justice. There is conceded to interested third parties the right to denounce the marriage to the Ordinary or the Promoter of Justice; thus they may inform the Ordinary or Promoter of Justice of the invalidity of the marriage, and the grounds on which the union may be impugned, thereby affording the Promoter of Justice an opportunity to impugn it.[22]

Non-Catholics, whether baptized or unbaptized, are also excluded from exercising the rôle of plaintiff in an ecclesiastical court unless permission of the Holy Office has first been asked and granted in each case.[23] Thus a non-Catholic, who had entered marriage, would be prevented from impugning a marriage in a formal trial unless the permission of the Holy Office had first been secured. The Catholic party would not be hindered by the fact that his consort had been or is a non-Catholic. All mixed marriages, however, which are brought in any way to the

---

[19] C. 1971; *1936 Instruction,* art. 35—*AAS,* XXVIII (1936), 313.

[20] *1936 Instruction,* art. 40—*AAS,* XXVIII (1936), 313.

[21] This right was forfeited by anyone who without legitimate cause remained silent about the impediment when he could have revealed it prior to the marriage. Cf. Wernz-Vidal, *Jus Matrimoniale,* n. 698, p. 834.

[22] *1936 Instruction,* art. 37, §4—*AAS,* XXVIII (1936), 313.

[23] S. C. S. O., 27 ian. 1928—*AAS,* XX (1928), 75; *Periodica,* XVII (1928), 54; Bouscaren, *Canon Law Digest,* I, 762, 763.

judicial cognizance of the Holy See, pertain to the Holy Office, since that congregation enjoys exclusive competence in any matrimonial case involving a non-Catholic.[24]

A further restriction of the right of the parties to impugn a marriage placed upon those parties who have been the culpable cause of the impediment.[25] The word "impediment" was used in canon 1971 of the Code and article 35 of the *1936 Instruction.* Ordinarily this term does not include the lack of canonical form of marriage, since clandestinity is not listed among the impediments to marriage in the Code. Canons 1058–1066 list those impediments which make a marriage unlawful, though not invalid, and canons 1067–1080 list the impediments invalidating a marriage. The form of marriage, however, is decreed in canons 1094, 1098, 1099. But the Pontifical Commission for the Interpretation of the Code decreed in 1929 that the word "impediment" in canon 1971 includes not only the impediments properly so-called, as enumerated in canons 1067–1080, but also the impediments improperly so-called, which are listed in canons 1080–1103.[26] The language of article 37 of the *1936 Instruction* follows this interpretation in declaring that a party to a marriage may not impugn its validity, if he has been the "culpable cause of the impediment *or of the nullity.*" [27]

In a common law marriage the party guilty of the nullity would be anyone who is bound to observe a formal procedure for entering the marriage, yet who knowingly and willingly fails to comply with the law, when its observance is possible.[28] Doheny is of the opinion that the restriction of the guilty party's right to impugn is in the nature of a penalty. "Our opinion is that the disqualification or restriction is of the nature of a penalty," he states. "Wherever grave culpability exists, there the law binds with full

---

[24] S. C. S. O., 27 ian. 1928—*loc. cit.*

[25] C. 1971; *1936 Instruction,* art. 35, §1, 1º—*AAS,* XXVIII (1936), 313.

[26] *PCI,* 12 martii 1929—*ASS,* XXI (1929), 171; Bouscaren, *Canon Law Digest,* I, 807.

[27] *1936 Instruction,* art. 37, §1—*AAS,* XXVIII (1936), 313.

[28] "A consort may be said to be the culpable cause of the impediment when he or she knowingly and willfully placed some obstacle calculated to render the marriage invalid."—Doheny, *Canonical Procedure in Matrimonial Cases,* p. 88.

force and the parties are estopped from acting as plaintiffs. This culpability may arise from fraud, deceit, malice, and the like or it may result from a wilful neglect in the observance of the Church's laws on marriage." [29]

This concept of the penal nature of the restriction seems to be correct, especially since the party who places an honest and licit cause of an impediment is not denied the right to attack the marriage which is invalid because of the placing of that impediment.[30] The culpable party, not the one who acts honestly and licitly, is punished. As an example, Doheny declares that a young man who marries before he has attained the canonical age for marriage is not the culpable cause of the impediment merely by virtue of the fact that he is not yet sixteen; such a young man might in good faith think he was capable of marrying validly according to the law of the Church. If, however, knowing that he was too young to marry validly, the young man were to conceal his true age, fraudulently or maliciously, and marry, he would then be the culpable cause of the impediment, and would be unable to impugn the marriage.[31]

Applying the same reasoning to a marriage case, which is brought to trial on the grounds of defective form, a person could not be plaintiff if he were culpable in omitting the prescribed form of marriage. Culpability in this case would arise from any ignorance which is vincible, that is, an ignorance which could have been dispelled by the use of moral diligence.[32] If a Catholic failed to attend church, and thereby remained in ignorance of the Church law requiring formalities for marriage, his ignorance of the law would be culpable; so too, if a Catholic doubted about the procedure necessary to enter marriage, and yet failed to re-

---

[29] Doheny, *op. cit.*, 88, 89.

[30] *PCI*, 17 iulii, 1933—*AAS*, XXV (1933), 345; also *1936 Instruction*, art. 37, §2—*AAS*, XXVIII (1936), 313.

[31] Doheny, *Canonical Procedure in Matrimonial Cases*, 89.

[32] Ignorance is defined by Cicognani as "the lack of due knowledge," and is contrasted by him to *inscience*, or "the lack of knowledge that a person is not required to have." This learned canonist further classifies ignorance as vincible "if it can be dispelled by the use of moral diligence; this is culpable and at least indirectly voluntary." Cicognani, *Canon Law*, 590, 591.

move that doubt by asking a priest or someone who would know the law of the Church, his ignorance would be vincible or culpable. Culpable ignorance of the law cannot be claimed as an excusing factor so as to allow the ignorant party the right to attack the marriage.[33]

Invincible ignorance of the Church law requiring a formal marriage would not, however, prevent a person from attacking his marriage which had been invalid because of its defective form. Invincible ignorance in the words of Cicognani is had "when a person is unable to rid himself of it, notwithstanding the use of moral diligence; obviously such ignorance is involuntary and not imputable." [34] Because ignorance of the law is generally not presumed,[35] the plaintiff who claims invincible ignorance must prove that he neither knows the law nor could have known it even though he used the prudent diligence that men ordinarily employ in transacting serious business. Since the Church laws against informal marriage, in existence since the Council of Trent, have been universally promulgated at least since 1908 (the date of the Decree *Ne temere*), it is readily seen that cases of true invincible ignorance on the point in question would be most rare. Yet since a person, in invincible ignorance of the Church law requiring formalities for marriage, might conceivably exist, it must be admitted that such a person would not be estopped from impugning as plaintiff his common law marriage by virtue of the prohibition of canon 1970 and article 37 of the *1936 Instruction.*

When a guilty party denounces the invalidity of his marriage to the Promoter of Justice, this latter can impugn the marriage only when the following conditions are verified:

1. The impediment must have become public. (In our case, this would mean that the nullity of the common law marriage were publicly known, because it is divulged that one of the

---

[33] For, according to canon 2229, §3, culpable ignorance, which is crass or supine, does not excuse from the incurring of a vindictive penalty imposed by law. Ignorance is said to be crass or supine, "when practically no effort is made to dispel it, because of heedlessness and laziness." Cf. Cicognani, *loc. cit.*

[34] Cicognani, *Canon Law,* 590, 591.

[35] C. 16.

parties, at least, was held to the observance of a prescribed form for marriage.)

2. The impediment must be supported by arguments so certainly and strongly established both in fact and in law that there can be no serious doubt about the existence or force of the impediment or cause of nullity. In a common law marriage, the lack of ecclesiastical validation of the marriage would constitute a strong argument for the nullity, so long as at least one of the parties was held to observe the canonical form of marriage.

3. The public good, namely, the removal of scandal, must demand the accusation, in the judgment of the Ordinary. This scandal must arise from the marriage under attack or from circumstances attendant upon it, not, however, from some later or subsequent marriage entered into by one of the parties to the invalid marriage.

If, as often happens, the parties to the marriage under attack have already separated, or have already obtained a civil divorce, their marriage no longer serves as an occasion of scandal. If under such circumstances, one of the parties seeks a declaration of nullity in order to contract a new marriage, or in order to validate a second marriage already entered with a third person, the public good would hardly demand the accusation of the first marriage, since the separation of the parties has already removed the cause of scandal, and the public good cannot be said to demand an accusation of a marriage which no longer causes scandal; such being true, the Promoter of Justice would be excluded from acting as plaintiff. The Ordinary, however, is to decide whether or not the public good has been sufficiently procured by the separation of the parties, and his judgment of such a problem is decisive and definitive.

A letter from the Apostolic Delegate to the United States stresses the fact that the Promoter of Justice will seldom impugn a marriage when the consorts are incapable of doing so. In this letter, Archbishop Cicognani stated: "Hence the case in which the Promoter of Justice can impugn the marriage, when the consorts are disqualified, is very rare indeed, not to say exceptional. The reason is that the Promoter of Justice, under the authority and guidance of the Bishop, can act solely to foster the public good.

And the public good demands that the culpable parties should not acquire freedom, as if in reward for their fault, but rather, *digna factis recipiant,* that they receive what is due their evil doing, and in this way serve as a warning to the rest of the faithful not to defile the celebration of Christian marriage with the exclusion of the *bona matrimonii* or with simulations of consent." [36]

4. Even upon the cessation of the impediment, the marriage could not be properly contracted. If marriage between the parties is possible when the impediment ceases, the Church strives rather to procure the validation of the union, as justice would thus best be served. For as Doheny points out,[37] the cohabitation of the parties which has thus far existed has established a certain identification between the parties, since cohabitation is normally the life of wedded persons.

Sometimes marriage will be impossible even after the cessation of the impediment. Thus in a common law marriage, the parties may be threatening to separate because of domestic discord, and in such a situation their perverse wills render impractical any attempt to celebrate marriage in the proper form.[38]

Since the prohibition against the party culpable of the cause of nullity holds in any court, it is required for validity that in the court of second instance, the Promoter of Justice act as plaintiff since the parties to the marriage cannot do so.[39]

ARTICLE 3. PROOF OF COMMON LAW MARRIAGE

To facilitate the treatment of this subject matter and in an endeavor to clarify a rather perplexing problem, this article will be divided so that the proofs admissible in the informal procedure will be discussed first; then will be treated the proofs allowable

---

36 Letter of Apostolic Delegate on Handling of Marriage Cases in the United States (Apostolic Delegation, U. S., 23 Sept. 1938), Private—Bouscaren, *The Canon Law Digest,* Suppl., p. 195.

37 *Canonical Procedure in Matrimonial Cases,* 98.

38 Cf. *1936 Instruction,* art. 39—*AAS,* XXVIII (1936), 313; Doheny, *op. cit.,* 96-98.

39 Dalpiaz, "An in altera instantia causae de qua in can. 1971, §1, n. 2, requiratur ad validitatem interventus promotoris iustitiae, etiamsi defensor vinculi appellationem interposuerit?"—*Apollinaris* (Romae, 1928-   ), VIII (1935), 139, 140.

in a formal marriage trial, first when that trial concerns a marriage in which at least one of the parties, through Baptism, is subject to the norms of Canon Law, and secondly, a trial in which neither party to the marriage under attack is baptized, but in which the ecclesiastical judge is competent by virtue of the fact that one of the parties to the marriage under attack now wishes to marry a Catholic.[40]

A. Proof Admissible in an Informal Procedure

The informal procedure for declaring a marriage null because of defective form can be used only when at least one party to the marriage is certainly bound to the canonical form of marriage, and yet has failed to observe that form.[41] Furthermore, proof in this process must be established beyond a question of doubt, for if doubt remains after prudent investigation, the question must be decided according to the ordinary procedure of law, i.e., by a solemn canonical trial. These requirements are demanded by article 231 of the *1936 Instruction.* Thus the informal procedure could be used whenever a Latin Catholic has failed to enter a formal marriage as the canons demand, but instead has entered a common law marriage. If the common law marriage is one which was entered according to the prescriptions of canon 1098, this procedure cannot be used if the marriage stands recorded as is demanded by canon 1103; for in such a case the marriage has been entered according to the less formal prescriptions of the canons.

The informal procedure would be available for any marriage entered by a Catholic which did not conform either to the prescriptions which demand the usual juridical form of marriage on the part of Catholics or to the prescriptions which obtain for those cases wherein the full formalities are impossible of observance. When all canonical provisions have been neglected, proof of the non-observance of these formalities may be discovered by a search of the records of those parishes or dioceses wherein it was possible for the couple to have had their marriage canonically celebrated, validated or healed through a dispensation

[40] Cf. *supra*, p. 98.

[41] *1936 Instruction*, art. 231—*AAS*, XXVIII (1936), 313, sqq.

from the form of marriage or through a *sanatio in radice.* Any ecclesiastical record which states that the marriage was canonically contracted also proves the existence of that marriage; for the marriage records in a parochial or diocesan registry, as well as all official copies or transcripts thereof, constitute public documents and accordingly afford full proof of the fact of marriage.[42] Similarly, the lack of registration of any such marriage attests the fact that such a marriage was not duly performed, and therefore the non-observance of canonical formalities may be established by a search of the ecclesiastical records. If the person to whose care these records are by law committed should draw up or sign a document attesting to the negative result of the search for the marriage record, such a document would afford adequate proof that no marriage had been duly contracted. For though the non-existence of a fact will not frequently be proved by a document, nevertheless an official document drawn up or signed by the legal custodian of an ecclesiastical register when he acted in his official capacity may afford proof equal to that of a document proving a positive fact.[43]

B. Proof Admissible in a Formal Trial

In judicial trials the existence of a marriage may be proved

---

[42] Canon 1812 mentions that proof by public document is admissible in any ecclesiastical trial, and therefore it seems but right that public documents be accepted without question in an informal procedure; canon 1813, §1, 4°, lists as public ecclesiastical documents: "inscriptiones . . . matrimonii . . . quae habentur in regestris Curiae vel paroeciae, vel religionis, et attestationes scriptae ex eisdem assumptae et a parochis, vel Ordinariis, vel notariis ecclesiasticis confectae aut earum exemplaria authentica."

Even though the facts entered on the marriage register depend on the testimony of the witnesses or of the parties to the marriage as often as the marriage has been entered according to the prescriptions of canon 1098, nevertheless the value of such records consists in the vigilance of the pastor or of the official who makes the entry, since he is bound by his office to enter in the record only those facts the veracity of which he can attest, and in fact does so attest by making the entry. Cf. Lega-Bartoccetti, *Commentarius in Iudicia Ecclesiastica* (3 vols., Romae: Anonima Libraria Cattolica Italiana, 1938–1941), II, 786.

[43] Cf. *PCI,* 16 iun. 1931, ad I—*AAS,* XXIII (1931), 353, 354; *Enchiridion Canonicum,* 360, 361.

by documentary evidence, by the testimony of witnesses, or in some cases by the testimony of the parties themselves. Inasmuch as a marriage in which at least one party is baptized must be adjudicated according to the norms of Canon Law, while a marriage of two unbaptized is subject to the legislative prescriptions of civil law, these two types of common law marriage will be treated separately. In either of these possible situations proof may be of the contract of marriage itself, or it may affirm only the status of marriage.

1. MARRIAGE IN WHICH AT LEAST ONE PARTY IS BAPTIZED

At the outset it must be remembered that not only all Latin Catholics but also the Catholics of some Oriental disciplines are bound to observe formalities in entering marriage, while baptized non-Catholics and the Catholics in certain Oriental disciplines are not held to the observance of any formalities in contracting marriage. For this latter group any mutual expression of true marital consent may constitute marriage.

For all baptized persons, however, the physical presence of the parties in the same place at the time of marriage either personally or by authorized proxy is demanded by canon 1088, §1. Through the employment of a duly authorized proxy a baptized person can contract marriage while he is separated from his partner in the celebration of the marriage. Canon 1088, §2, ordains that the couple entering the marriage should express their consent in words; therefore, any other means or form of expressing that consent is illegal, though the marriage could still be valid. The exemption from the Catholic form of marriage, granted to baptized non-Catholics,[44] does not extend to the prescriptions of canon 1088, since this canon is not listed in the Code among those canons which decree the form of marriage, but rather it is found among those canons which determine the necessity of consent, and it therefore comes under those canons concerning which Nau states: "The Church has enacted for the baptized certain laws which declare and define more explicitly the requirements of the natural law and has moreover added thereunto other requirements

[44] C. 1099, §2.

to more fully protect the free choice of the contract." [45] It seems that the prescriptions of canon 1088 also extend to Orientals, even though they be not bound by the form of marriage as expressed in the Code.

(a) *Proving the Contract of Marriage*

Documentary evidence of the contract of marriage is rare in a common law marriage. However, since the term "common law marriage" as used in civil law admits of connotations other than a mere clandestine union, the possibility of documentary proof of such a marriage cannot be overlooked.

Common law marriage includes, besides a union which is secret or clandestine, those marital unions which were formally entered, but invalidly so because of the incompetency of the officiating minister,[46] or because of the presence of some diriment impediment, and which after the cessation of the impediment were validated by the continuing consent of the parties. As Koegel remarks: "The general rule in a State recognizing common law marriage is that the continued cohabitation of the parties after the removal of the impediment to a valid ceremonial marriage constitutes a common law marriage, and in a few jurisdictions marriages under such circumstances are recognized, although common law marriages as such are invalid." [47]

The Church admits no such validation of a marriage by mere continuance of consent or cohabitation. While the fact that a marriage was entered gives rise to a presumption of its validity,[48] the continuance of a union which was invalid at the start does not render the union valid. If some impediment had hindered the validity of the marriage, then upon the cessation of that impediment a new contract would have to be entered, by a new act of the will of both parties, or at least of the one who knew of the existence of the impediment, before the marriage would be ca-

---

[45] Nau, *Manual on the Marriage Laws of the Code of Canon Law,* n. 98, pp. 121, 122.

[46] The term "minister" is here used in its generic sense to include a priest or civil official, as well as a minister of a non-Catholic sect.

[47] Koegel, *Common Law Marriage,* p. 153.

[48] C. 1014.

nonically valid.[49] If defective consent had impeded the validity of the marriage, otherwise formally valid, the renewal of consent by that party who had not truly consented would be required and would suffice to render the marriage valid,[50] provided that the consent of the other party perseveres. If the defect of consent was external at the beginning of the marriage, then the renewal of consent must be made externally; if proof of this external renewal of consent were not adduced in a marriage in which it was required, the continued cohabitation of the parties does not afford any presumption that the marriage is a valid one. Thus if the marriage contract of a Catholic is invalid because one of the parties did not externally manifest his consent during the celebration of the marriage according to the prescribed juridical form, then the marriage itself is invalid. No matter how long the appearances of marriage are maintained, that external defect in the expression of consent—which would be equivalent to the lack of proper form inasmuch as an essential part of the form was omitted—continues to exist, and the marriage does not become validated until the consent is actually expressed in the proper canonical form, namely in the presence of a duly authorized priest and two attendant witnesses. Documentary proof of the renewal of consent in the external forum should be sought, then, in the marriage register of the parish or diocese wherein the marriage was contracted. If such proof is lacking, no presumption of validity should be accorded to the marriage.

Another instance in which documentary proof of the contract of common law marriage is available is had in the case of a marriage contracted according to the prescriptions of canon 1098. A marriage of this kind, since it was performed without the full solemnities of the Catholic ritual and without the assistance of a qualified witness authorized by ecclesiastical law to assist at marriage, is according to the terminology of civil law a common law marriage, provided of course that none of the witnesses to the marriage was authorized by civil law to accept or receive the consent of the parties. Thus a marriage before witnesses alone may be a formal civil marriage if one of the witnesses was accredited

---

[49] Cc. 1133, 1134.
[50] C. 1136.

in civil law as a competent person for witnessing civil marriages, v. gr., a justice of the peace, or a priest not canonically authorized to assist. Ordinarily, however, such marriages are regarded as non-ceremonial in the eyes of the civil law, inasmuch as they do not conform to the requisites of a formal marriage.

Canon law provides for the registration of such marriages by placing an obligation on a priest, if he be present, and on the witnesses conjointly with the parties to the marriage, of seeing to it that the marriage be recorded in the parochial or diocesan register.[51] The ecclesiastical record of such a marriage would afford full proof that the marriage was celebrated, and, similarly, the lack of such a record would indicate conclusively that the marriage had not been performed.[52]

For baptized non-Catholics, for whom no form of marriage is required, proof of the contract of marriage can be established by a document provided that the parties expressed their consent in writing in each other's presence. This document, if signed by a notary, constitutes a public document; as such it affords full proof of the marriage.[53] If the written evidence of matrimonial consent is afforded by a private document, such as a contract signed by the parties only, then such a document affords full proof of the marriage, provided that it stands proved as genuine, i.e., not forged, mutilated or garbled. For though any letter, document or contract executed by private persons is not a public, but rather a private document,[54] yet, when it is acknowledged by

---

[51] C. 1103, §3. The registration which seemingly, according to the text of the law, may be made either in the records of the parish where the marriage took place, or in the records of the parish where ordinarily the marriage should have occurred, is, according to the more common opinion, to be recorded in the parish (or diocese, if no parish exists) where the marriage was contracted. Cf. O'Rourke, *Parish Registers,* The Catholic University of America Canon Law Studies, n. 88 (Washington, D. C.: The Catholic University of America, 1934), 73.

[52] Cf. *supra,* p. 107.

[53] C. 1813, §1, 2°, which declares that a public document is one which is drawn up by an ecclesiastical notary; §2 of the same canon declares that a civil public document is any document which is recognized as such according to the civil law of the place wherein it is drawn up. Civil laws recognize as public those documents which are signed by a notary public.

[54] C. 1813, §3.

its author as his own writing or when it is accepted as genuine by the judge, it furnishes proof against the author.[55] Consequently, in any matrimonial trial, wherein a marriage is impugned, if a letter expressing matrimonial consent be adduced as evidence against the one who denies the existence of the marriage, the fact that he wrote the letter or contract which expresses his matrimonial consent therein furnishes proof against his present contention that he never entered the marriage.[56]

American civil law has recognized as valid a marriage which is entered by document or letter, though such recognition is usually, though not entirely, reserved to those jurisdictions which recognize common law marriage as valid.[57]

In defect of documentary proof of the contract of marriage, the testimony of witnesses can prove that matrimonial consent was exchanged between the parties. Though the case would be a rare one, witnesses who heard the parties pledge themselves one to the other as man and wife could afford full proof of that fact; the concordant testimony of two witnesses above exception would of course be required.[58] If contrary indications in the case should engender a doubt about the assertions of the witnesses, it is within the province of the judge to demand further proof.[59] However, the denial by either or both of the married parties does

---

[55] C. 1817.

[56] Thus the Roman Rota recognized as valid under pre-Code law the matrimonial consent of a groom, when his letter which expressed his consent to the marriage had been read in the presence of the bride's pastor and two witnesses; S. R. R., *Nullitas matrimonii,* coram R. P. D. Gustavo Persiani, 19 ian. 1910, dec. III—*Decisiones* II (1910), 19–32; *AAS,* II (1910), 297–309.

[57] "In many American jurisdictions the assent of parties capable of contracting marriage is all that is required to a valid marriage and that consent need not be expressed before any religious or civil celebrant. In such a jurisdiction if two persons exchange letters wherein *per verba de praesenti* they take each other as husband and wife they are legally married." These words from an editorial in 22 Law Notes (1919) are quoted in Koegel, *Common Law Marriage,* 133; cf. also p. 131.

[58] C. 1791, §2; Whalen, *The Value of Testimonial Evidence in Matrimonial Procedure,* The Catholic University of America Canon Law Studies, n. 99 (Washington, D. C.: The Catholic University of America, 1935), pp. 251–253.

[59] C. 1791, §2.

not effectively contradict the legitimate depositions of acceptable witnesses.[60]

In defect of registration of the marriage and of witnesses to the expression of consent, the testimony of the parties assumes prime importance. If both parties under oath affirm the fact of marriage, their assertions must be believed except when their testimony is prejudicial to a former marriage publicly contracted. If one of the parties had previously publicly contracted marriage with a third party, his later common law marriage would not be sufficiently proved by the mere testimony of the parties themselves, unless it could be proved the former public marriage was certainly invalid.[61] If full proof be not required, e.g., if no other marriage were prejudiced by the assertions of the parties, their sworn statements may be accepted as proof of their marriage and of the legitimacy of their children.[62]

If both parties under oath deny that they ever contracted marriage, their testimony, in defect of other proof, will suffice to establish their freedom to marry.[63]

If one party affirms the common law marriage, while the other party denies it, the burden of proof rests on the one who asserts that marriage was contracted.[64]

In the face of contradictory assertions of the parties concerning the fact of marriage, the status of marriage will usually be advanced as indicative or presumptive of the fact that the contract of marriage was entered.

(b) *The Status of Marriage as Proof*

In the eyes of the civil law, proof of common law marriage usually depends upon the assumption of the marital status by the parties. In fact it may be said that the assumption of the marital status is requisite for common law marriage, unless the contract

[60] Wernz-Vidal, *Ius Matrimoniale,* n. 580, p. 679.

[61] Wernz-Vidal, *Ius Matrimoniale,* n. 580, p. 687.

[62] S. C. Sacr., 6 mart. 1911—*AAS,* III (1911), 103; Payen, *De Matrimonio,* II, n. 1930, p. 303.

[63] C. 1, X, *de sponsalibus et matrimonio,* IV, 1; Wernz, *Ius Decretalium,* Vol. IV (*Ius Matrimoniale*), pars 1, n. 187, pp. 281, 282.

[64] C. 28, X, *de sponsalibus et matrimonio,* IV, 1; Wernz, *ibid., in nota* 257.

be capable of proof in writing or some equally certain manner. For the courts have held as a matter of general policy: (1) That some public recognition of the marriage is necessary as evidence of its existence;[65] (2) that this public recognition may be present in any way which can be perceived;[66] (3) that a single act of public recognition suffices, and that no continuance or repetition of it is required.[67] Once a man and woman have given evidence that they treated and considered each other as man and wife, civil law in those states which recognize common law marriages as valid presumes the couple to be properly married. While cohabitation and the repute of marital status are not constitutive of marriage—and this principle is recognized in civil law[68]—yet they are taken as indicative of the existence of the marriage contract, and are productive then of a presumption of marriage. The cohabitation as man and wife may give rise to the presumption that an actual marriage has been contracted, even though no documentary evidence of direct testimony thereof exists. This presumption of the contraction marriage, in the absence of any evidence in rebuttal, may be considered conclusive of the fact

[65] "To insure the protection of the parties and their children and upon consideration of sound public policy, some public recognition of the marriage is necessary as evidence of its existence."—Matter of Seymour, 113 Misc. 421, 423, 185 N. Y. S. 373; 38 C. J. §93, p. 1318.

[66] "This public recognition may be made in any way which can be seen and known by men, such as living together as man and wife, or by public conduct which acknowledges the relation."—Sorenson v. Sorenson, 68 Nebr. 483, 509, 94 N. W. 540—38 C. J. §93, p. 1318.

[67] "The law does not require that they live together at all after the contract of marriage is made to render the marriage a valid one . . . A single act of consummation and a single act of recognition would be competent to support the contention that the parties constituted and actually entered into a marriage contract."—Davidson v. Ream, 97 Misc. 89, 111, 161 N. Y. S. 73; affd. 178 App. Div. 362, 164 N. Y. S. 1037—38 C. J. §93, p. 1318.

[68] "Marriage and cohabitation are two things. The latter is the object of the former, and to make it lawful, must be preceded by the former. It is said, indeed, that a marriage contracted *per verba de futuro,* which is in truth nothing but a promise to marry in future, is a valid marriage if the parties afterward cohabit; but the cohabitation, even in that case, does not constitute the marriage. It is only evidence of the marriage . . ."—Dumaresly v. Fishly, 10 Ky. 368; in Koegel, *Common Law Marriage,* 121, 122.

that marriage was contracted. The presumption, however, may always be rebutted, and it wholly disappears in the face of proof that no marriage in fact has taken place.[69]

In ecclesiastical jurisprudence two kinds of presumption[70] are recognized, namely, those which are predetermined in the law itself and those which are formulated by a judge. The former, the presumption of law, may be a *simple* presumption, which admits direct rebuttal, or it may be a presumption *in the law and by the law,* which does not admit of direct rebuttal and thus remains irrefutable except through a successful impugnment of the juridical fact which forms a basis for the presumption. A presumption of law releases from the burden of proof, and unless it is overthrown it forms the basis of a necessary decision in favor of the party who enjoys that presumption.[71]

At one time canonical jurisprudence recognized the possible existence of a presumed marriage which was based on a presumption *in the law and by the law.* Pope Alexander III (1159–1181) decreed that formal nuptial promises, *sponsalia de futuro,* followed by carnal marriage constituted marriage.[72] Shortly thereafter Gregory IX (1227–1241) declared that, if a man and woman had concluded a formal agreement to marry in the future, and had subsequently had sexual relations with each other, the Church would presume by an irrefutable presumption that the parties were married, and that the act of sexual intercourse had given present manifestation of the marital consent which had been pledged to become operative in the future. So strong was this presumption that a formal marriage, which amid ecclesiastical ceremonies was subsequently contracted by the man with another woman, could not militate against it. Despite his second

---

[69] 38 C. J. §98, pp. 1321, 1322; 38 C. J. §111, p. 1339.

[70] Canon 1825, §1, defines presumption as a probable conjecture on an uncertain issue; as Wanenmacher points out, the value of a presumption may be variable and it "depends on whether the probable conjecture rises in effect above probability and attains to moral certainty."—*Canonical Evidence in Marriage Cases* (Philadelphia: Dolphin Press, 1935), n. 384, p. 239.

[71] Cc. 1825–1827.

[72] C. 15, X, *de sponsalibus et matrimonio,* IV, 1.

wedding *in facie ecclesiae* the man was compelled to return to the first woman.[73]

This inevitable legal presumption of marriage may be traced back to Roman law for its foundation. For Justinian points out that a betrothal followed by *coitus* is marriage.[74] At face value, this presumption seems to contradict the constant teaching of the Church that marital consent alone constitutes marriage, and that no human power can supply for the deficiency of that consent.[75] Freisen inferred that the Papal Decretals of Alexander III and Gregory IX derived the presumption of marriage from the frequency of secret marriages in those times, and sanctioned the presumption by constituting betrothals followed by carnal relations as a diriment impediment to any subsequent marriage by either of the betrothed parties.[76] Wanenmacher points out that the presumption probably arose as a juridical effort to curb moral abuses, and that it rested "on the assumption that if, in such circumstances, marital consent is not presumed, fornication must be presumed, and to this presumption of crime the Church is not easily inclined." [77]

With the introduction of the law requiring a formal marriage for Catholics by the decrees *Tametsi* and *Ne temere* and by the Code, presumptive marriage was and is no longer admissible for Catholics. Pope Leo XIII totally abrogated this presumption so that it no longer exists, not even as a simple presumption of law.[78]

Concerning the presumptive force of the appearance of marriage, that is, of the repute of marital status derived from cohabitation, for Catholics it must be maintained that unless some *species* of a marriage contract has been observed, the marriage does not enjoy the presumed existence which canon 1014 interposes by its enunciation of the principle that "marriage enjoys the favor of law." This canon sets up a presumption that once the fact of marriage is present, the law will presume until the

[73] C. 30, X, *de sponsalibus et matrimonio*, IV, 1.

[74] Nov. 74.

[75] C. 1081, §1; Wanenmacher, *op. cit.*, n. 427, p. 273.

[76] Freisen, *Geschichte des canonischen Eherechts*, pp. 209–211.

[77] Wanenmacher, *Canonical Evidence in Marriage Cases*, n. 427, p. 273.

[78] Leo XIII, const. *Consensus mutuus*, 15 febr. 1892—*Collectanea*, n. 1279; *Fontes*, n. 613.

contrary is proved that the marriage is valid. It is not in accord with justice that the fact of marriage be presumed; otherwise any person could prevent another from entering marriage merely by stating that that other had already entered marriage. Thus if, when a man is about to enter marriage, a woman should approach the pastor and claim that she was already married to the man and that therefore he is not free to enter the presently proposed marriage, her statement of itself would not be accorded the presumption of canon 1014. If it were, the way would be opened to a situation in which every person entering marriage could be called upon to prove that he was not already married, each time that someone asserted that he was.

The rule of canon 1748, §1, states that the burden of proof rests with the person who makes the assertion. There is no trouble in applying this rule in a trial concerning the validity of a marriage, *once the fact of marriage is admitted.* The plaintiff who denies the validity of the marriage is he who asserts that some impediment hindered the valid contraction of the marriage; he must prove his assertion, namely that the alleged impediment really existed. Nor is there any difficulty in applying the same rule if the plaintiff sues to establish the *fact* of marriage. As plaintiff he must sustain the burden of proof and prove that the marriage was entered. However, it can happen that the plaintiff may deny the *fact* of marriage. For example, a reputed common law marriage, i.e., so reputed in the opinion of neighbors, is alleged by someone as an impeding factor to a marriage about to be entered by the plaintiff; he, in attempting to prove his present freedom to marry, could deny the existence of the alleged common law marriage. In other words, he denies the *fact* of marriage. He does not admit the fact of marriage and base his plaint on the grounds that some impediment co-existed with the celebration of the marriage to hinder the valid contraction of the marriage; he denies that a real marriage, i.e., one in the eyes of canon law, took place. In reality then, it is the defendant who claims that the marriage occurred; it is the defendant who makes the assertion and, so it seems according to canon 1748, §1, he must sustain the burden of proof. For in such a case the plaintiff's plea of the non-existence of marriage is based, in the terminology of Wanenmacher, "on a negation of law (*negativum juris*) wherein it is denied that a thing has been done according to law." And as Wanenmacher states: "If the thing or act whose legality or validity is denied belongs to the class of things in general forbidden, v. gr., clandestine marriage, the burden of proof devolves upon him who asserts the legality or validity in a particular case." [79]

The Roman Rota, in a case tried in 1909, declared that sometimes it is equitable to depart from the presumption of law: "*In dubio standum est pro validitate matrimonii,*" and as an example of a case in which it is equitable to depart from that presumption it is stated: "Nam si a iuris praesumptione '*in dubio standum est pro validitate matrimonii,*' aliquando recedere aequum est, quando nimirum quaestio agitur de facto, utrum scilicet matrimonium fuerit unquam contractum necne, in praesenti," etc.[80]

From this decision Chelodi argued that, even under the law of the Code, as often as a truly clandestine marriage occurs, the marriage is not presumed to exist as a true marriage, but that inasmuch as it is something odious in law it must be proved.[81]

For a common law marriage, then, in which at least one of the parties is a Catholic, it must be stated that no matter how certainly the repute of marital status or the appearance of marriage is proved, unless there exists some record or registration of the marriage in the ecclesiastical records, or unless the formal marriage can be proved in some other certain manner, the common law marriage enjoys no presumption of validity and must be considered a sinful alliance.

---

[79] Wanenmacher, *Canonical Evidence in Marriage Cases,* n. 142, p. 85. That the burden of proof may sometimes rest on the defendant instead of on the plaintiff is admitted by Lega, *De Iudiciis Ecclesiasticis* (2 ed., 2 vols., Romae: Ex Typographia Polyglotta, 1905), I, n. 444, pp. 395–396; and Roberti, *De Processibus* (2 vols. in 1, Romae: Apud Aedes Facultatis Iuridicae Ad S. Apollinaris, 1926), II, n. 226, p. 28.

[80] S. R. R., *Nullitas matrimonii,* 28 maii 1909, coram R. P. D. Aloysio Sincero, dec. VI, n. 12—*Decisiones,* I (1909), 58. The Rota in arguing that it is sometimes equitable to depart from the presumption of the validity of a marriage, stated that it drew this argument from a decree of the Holy Office under date of Dec. 18, 1872. This decree is found in the *Collectanea,* n. 1392.

[81] Chelodi, *Ius Matrimoniale,* n. 7, p. 8.

If, on the contrary, no Catholic is involved in the marriage, but at least one of the parties has been validly baptized, the well grounded repute of marital status will give rise to the presumption that a valid contract has been entered. If the parties have held each other out in public as man and wife, if certain proof exists that they have cohabited as man and wife (not in a meretricious union or concubinage), then their status of marriage gives rise to the presumption that a valid marital contract has been entered. Since for baptized non-Catholics there is no requirement of a specific juridical form in the celebration of their marriage, a common law marriage on their part would not constitute an odious issue in the eyes of the Church's law, and therefore the presumption of canon 1014 would be validly applied by presuming their marriage to be valid.

The presumption that the couple is married may be established from any one or several of the following circumstances: The man and woman register as man and wife at a hotel or public place; the man and woman have a joint bank account, on which their names appear as man and wife; they file a joint income tax, as is done by a married couple; in the presence of third persons they treat each other and speak of each other as man and wife; one of the parties mentions the other as husband or as wife, as the beneficiary of an insurance policy. Any one of these facts is indicative of the fact that the parties have accepted each other as man and wife. And since for them there existed no requirement of any specific form in the celebration of their marriage, their assumption of the marital status must be presumed as indicative of true marital consent until the contrary stands proved.

Therefore the parties are presumed to have cohabited with marital intent rather than with sinful intent, and if the case at hand does not demand full proof, the presumptive force of their assumed status suffices to form the conclusion that they were married.

If, however, full proof be demanded, as, e.g., in the case wherein the common law marriage would prejudice another, formal marriage, the mere presumption would not suffice. For in marrying later in accord with a formal ceremony, the man who previously entered a clandestine union implicitly admits the wrongfulness or sinfulness of his first union. The certain proof of the formally contracted marriage establishes the later marriage as a certain fact, a fact which, once it is established, enjoys the presumption of validity according to the principle of canon 1014.[82] If the formally contracted marriage had preceded the clandestine union, the former of these marriages would be held as valid until it is proved null; if it is proved null, then the subsequent common law marriage could be and should be presumed as valid. If two successive common law marriages are encountered, it seems that, if no other decisive factor is present, the first of these marriages must be recognized as valid by way of presumption. While it is true that in any trial involving two successive common law unions a certain perplexity would be experienced by the court from the fact that each of the two marriages as taken up by the court enjoys the presumption of validity; yet the decision concerning the second marriage must be held in abeyance until the validity or nullity of the first is determined. Once it is proved that the status of marriage was assumed, the validity of the earlier marriage must be maintained until its invalidity is established by proof which rules out the presumed validity. Consequently the extant presumed validity for the bond of the existing marriage impedes the celebration of a subsequent marriage, and whatever presumption of validity may rest with the second marriage must yield to the presumption which favors the existence of the impediment of the prior bond (*ligamen*), for this impediment must logically be considered as present as long as the presumption of validity rests with the prior marriage.

2. MARRIAGE IN WHICH NEITHER PARTY IS BAPTIZED

The marriage of two infidels must be adjudged according to the legislation in force in the place where the marriage was contracted. Thus if the law of State requires a formal ceremony for the contraction of a valid marriage, the parties cannot enter a valid common law marriage. The Holy See apparently implies that custom also may legislate for the non-baptized, for in a re-

[82] Wanenmacher, *Canonical Evidence in Marriage Cases,* n. 485, pp. 311–314.

cent decision it has asked whether Chinese infidels in the Dutch East Indies, who contract marriage according to the manner of the Chinese, marry invalidly in the face of laws requiring certain formalities, obligatory in the Dutch East Indies. The reply was that the marriages were not certainly invalid under the circumstances, and it was declared that upon conversion such infidels should renew the matrimonial consent at least *ad cautelam.*[83] In the light of this response the Holy Office apparently was not certain whether some custom, privilege, or particular law would allow the Chinese to marry according to their own manner. In any event the reply, since it fails to state conclusively whether the marriages were valid or invalid, does not form the basis of proof either for or against the competency of civil laws or customs over infidels.

As previously stated, civil authority is competent to legislate for the unbaptized, so that their common law marriage must be adjudged according to their proper law. However, as the judge must have moral certitude in rendering judgment in a canonical trial,[84] the decisions of civil courts cannot be taken at face value as conclusive evidence. Rather the ecclesiastical judge should hear the arguments of the case. But for his purpose the recorded proceedings of the civil trial may be admitted as evidence and may go far towards facilitating the presentation and adjudication of the case.

Proof of the contract of marriage among infidels may be adduced in any of the manners indicated for the baptized,[85] but also the further possibility that the unbaptized may contract marriage while not in each other's presence must be considered.

American civil law has recognized as valid marriages which were contracted by document or by letter, though such recognition is usually, though not entirely, reserved to those jurisdictions which recognize common law marriage as valid.[86]

---

[83] Holy Office, 23 June 1938 (Private)—Bouscaren, *Canon Law Digest*, Suppl., pp. 121, 122.

[84] C. 1869, §1, 2.

[85] Cf. *supra*, pp. 109–113.

[86] "In many of the American jurisdictions the assent of parties capable of contracting marriage is all that is required to a valid marriage and that

During World War I the U. S. War Department assisted in the preparation and transmission of documents whereby soldiers in Europe contracted marriage with girls in America. These marriages were held valid, if the bride lived in a state recognizing mere consent as constitutive of marriage.[87] These documents were drawn up and signed by the respective parties in the presence of witnesses and of a notary public, thus giving them the force of public civil documents. Any public civil document is in canon law accepted as full proof of the facts it expresses.[88]

If marital consent were exchanged by means of a private letter or document, such a writing would afford only as much proof as the judge would attribute to it. If the letter were both genuine and credible, a judge, according to his discretion and in accord with the circumstances of the case, could attribute the force of full proof to it.[89]

If common law marriage is forbidden in a state, its legality in that state must be proved, not assumed; in such instances the burden of proof rests with the person who asserts the marriage. Furthermore, in such a state the status of marriage affords no presumption of validity for a marriage in the celebration of which there has been no compliance with the formal requisites of law.

Some states, while forbidding common law marriage within their jurisdiction, recognize the validity of such a union provided that the parties exchange consent in a state which does recognize common law marriage. Proof of this exchange of consent can be afforded by documentary evidence, by oral testimony, or by the presumption arising from the assumption of the marital status

---

consent need not be expressed before any religious or civil celebrant. In such a jurisdiction if two persons exchange letters wherein *per verba de praesenti* they take each other as husband and wife they are legally married." These words from an editorial in 22 Law Notes (1919) are quoted from Koegel, *Common Law Marriage*, 133.

[87] Koegel, *op. cit.*, p. 133.

[88] C. 1813, §2: "Documenta publica civilia ea sunt quae secundum uniuscuiusque loci leges talia iure censentur."

C. 1816: "Documenta publica fidem faciunt de iis quae directe et principaliter in eisdem affirmantur."

[89] C. 1753; Wanenmacher, *Canonical Evidence in Matrimonial Cases*, n. 380, pp. 385–386; cf. *supra*, pp. 109–113.

provided that this presumption is not overthrown by proof to the contrary.

If the civil law permits the sanation of an invalid marriage by the mere presence of the parties in a jurisdiction recognizing common law marriage,[90] proof of this sanation entails the establishment of two facts, namely of the original marriage contract and of the presence of the parties in a territory recognizing common law marriage. If an invalidating impediment had caused the invalidity of the marriage which is now to be validated, proof must be adduced to show that the impediment has ceased to exist, or at least has ceased to bind the parties in this case, at the time when the sanation is effected.

If the law of a state permits either the contraction of a common law marriage or the validation of an invalid union through the continued cohabitation of the parties the ecclesiastical judge must consider the marriage status as he would that of baptized non-Catholics, as previously explained.[91] In other words, inasmuch as the marriage or its sanation is permissible at law, it will be presumed valid or sanated (as the case may be) as long as evidence is adduced to show that the parties have by word or by act accepted each other as man and wife in any jurisdiction recognizing common law marriage.

---

[90] Cf. *supra*, pp. 7–8.

[91] Cf. *supra*, pp. 119–120.

CHAPTER IX

Penalties for Attempted Common Law Marriages

To safeguard the sanctity of marriage and thereby the more effectively to procure the salvation of souls, the Church has decreed certain penalties for violation of her matrimonial laws. Some marriages are prohibited because they entail an association of Catholics with heretics or schismatics in the manifestation of the practices and tenets of the latters' religion; some because they violate the free exercise of the human will; some because they import the improper reception of the Sacrament, and others because they violate obligations proper to a certain state of life, such as the clerical or religious state. While common law marriage differs but little from a ceremonial marriage in the incurring of some of these penalties, the problem of penalties incurred by those who attempt common law marriages will be treated briefly.

Common law marriage, since of itself it does not associate the parties with an heretical or schismatical sect, does not entail the punishment of excommunication which is meted out to those who enter marriage before a non-Catholic minister.[1] If, however, a man and woman enter common law marriage with a pact, either explicit or implied, to educate any or all of their children outside of the Catholic religion, the parties are at the moment of marriage excommunicated from the communion of the faithful in the Church.[2] If the pact were made to educate the children in the public schools of the United States, which teach no religion whatsoever, and without any view to supplementing this non-religious education with some Catholic training either in the home or elsewhere, the penalty would be incurred; education in a non-Catholic religion is not demanded that this censure be incurred, and if

[1] C. 2319, §1, 1º.

[2] C. 2319, §1, 2º.

the children were reared with no religious education, they would most certainly be educated outside of the Catholic Church. This excommunication is reserved by law to the Ordinary.

A similar excommunication is incurred by those parties to a common law marriage who presume to present their children to a non-Catholic minister for Baptism, or who knowingly have their children brought up, or instructed in a non-Catholic religion. Even though the common law marriage were an invalid union, the penalty would still be incurred, for the canon levying the penalty mentions the "parents," without specifying the necessity of a canonical or valid marriage on the part of these parents.[3] This excommunication is incurred by the Catholic party in the marriage, and since the canon requires full knowledge of the act, any ignorance, except simulated or affected ignorance, of the law, its penalty, or of the facts of the case excuses from the incurring of the penalty.[4]

If, under the pretext of taking a woman as his common law wife, a man should abduct a woman, or if he should elope with a girl under the age of twenty-one against the wishes or knowledge of her parents, he is penalized by being automatically excluded from performing any "legitimate acts" in the Church.[5] This provision of the penal law is enacted to safeguard the liberty of women in entering marriage, and to protect them from the moral depredations of immoral men. Civil laws usually provide heavy penalties for this offense, and in the United States the crime is punishable not only when a man abducts a woman for the purpose of marrying her himself, but also if he does so to facilitate her marriage with another man.[6]

A man or woman, who has a wife or husband yet living, and who nevertheless attempts a common law marriage with another person, becomes infamous in view of such an attempted marriage, and should be warned by the Ordinary to quit the illegal

---

[3] C. 2319, §1, 3°, 4°; Cocchi, *Commentarium in Codicem Iuris Canonici* (5 vols. in 8), VIII, *De Delictis et Poenis* (4 ed., Taurini: Marietti, 1938), nn. 149, 150, p. 237.

[4] C. 2229, §1–2; Cocchi, *loc. cit.*

[5] C. 2353.

[6] Alford, *Jus Matrimoniale Comparatum*, n. 239, p. 170.

and sinful union; if the warning falls on heedless ears, the culprit may be excommunicated or personally interdicted, and if no signs of repentance are forthcoming before the death of the culprit, he is to be denied Christian burial.[7] Furthermore, in the United States those who attempt marriage while they are already bound by the bond of a prior marriage incur an excommunication reserved to the Ordinary, by virtue of a decree of the III Plenary Council of Baltimore.[8] This censure, still binding under the law of the Code, also presupposes a full knowledge of the law, of the penalty, and of the facts of the case, before the penalty will be incurred.

Another penalty of the Code, destined to protect the freedom of young girls, is decreed in canon 2357 of the Code, which declares infamous a man convicted of the crime of sins against the Sixth Commandment with a girl under sixteen. Included among the sins mentioned specifically in this canon are rape and incest. Wherefore, if under pretext of a common law marriage a layman commits any of these sins, and is convicted of his crime in civil court, he becomes infamous in the eyes of the Church law and as such is irregular or impeded from the reception of Orders,[9] is incapable of receiving any office, pension, benefice or dignity in the Church, and of performing "legitimate acts" in the Church, of exercising any ecclesiastical right or office, and finally he must be restrained from the exercise of the ministry in sacred functions.[10] If, of course, a valid common law marriage is entered, as, v. gr., according to canon 1098, the possibility of the incurring of this penalty remains slight, since sexual sins among married persons are seldom touched by civil law; but if such were true, and if civil conviction for such a sin were had, this penalty would be incurred automatically. This penalty is for laymen only, since the penalty against clerics is legislated in canons which follow and which will be treated shortly.

---

[7] C. 2356, 1240, §1, 6°; Cocchi, *De Delictis et Poenis*, n. 210, p. 314.

[8] N. 124—*Acta et Decreta Concilii Plenarii Baltimorensis Tertii* (Baltimorae, 1886), pp. 124, 125; Beste, *Introductio in Codicem* (Collegeville, Minn.: St. John's Abbey Press, 1938), p. 958.

[9] C. 984, §5.

[10] C. 2294.

A common law marriage, which is adulterous or which, in the eyes of the Church, is but public concubinage, entails for the baptized parties of such a union exclusion from all legitimate ecclesiastical acts. This exclusion is terminated only when the parties have given true signs of repentance.[11]

Clerics who attempt a common law marriage are guilty of a civilly attempted marriage if the state in which the marriage is attempted recognizes common law marriage as valid. For a common law marriage fulfills the requisities of a civil marriage in those states. Most of the authors agree that a civil marriage is one which is contracted in accordance with the requisites of civil laws,[12] though some define a civil marriage as one which is entered before a civil magistrate.[13] However, this latter group seems not to advert to the possibility of a twofold legal system of common law and of statute law such as is had in the United States. Furthermore, any attempted marriage by a cleric in sacred orders, or by a religious with a solemn vow of chastity, incurs for them and for those contracting marriage with them, the penalty of excommunication reserved to the Holy See; if clerics guilty of this crime do not heed the warning of their Ordinary and do not amend within the time defined by the Ordinary, they are to be degraded; finally, if the crime be committed by a religious whose vow of chastity is perpetual but only simple, the excommunication is incurred but its absolution is reserved to the Ordinary.[14] Since state laws have no binding force on baptized persons when they decree a form necessary for the entrance of marriage, it seems that a common law marriage attempted in those states which do not recognize such marriages as valid would likewise furnish a basis for the penalty just mentioned. For canon 2388 states that the penalty is incurred for the attempt of marriage. And the Holy Office declared in pre-Code law that it made no difference whether defective form or some other impedi-

[11] C. 2357, §2.

[12] Payen, *De Matrimonio,* I, n. 130, pp. 96, 97; Cappello, *De Sacramentis,* III, pars 1, n. 49, p. 54; Alford, *Jus Matrimoniale Comparatum,* n. 31, pp. 21, 22.

[13] Wernz-Vidal, *Ius Matrimoniale,* n. 580, pp. 680, 681; Coronata, *Institutiones Iuris Canonici,* IV, n. 2194, p. 633.

[14] C. 2388.

ment caused the nullity of the marriage.[15] Therefore, any attempted marriage implies the incurring of the penalty listed in canon 2388. Even in those states which deny the validity of common law marriage, it is certain that, for baptized persons, such laws lack competency, and therefore are to be disregarded in any canonical evaluation of a common law marriage entered by a baptized person.

To incur the excommunication of canon 2388, true matrimonial consent must be given. Sole,[16] Cappello[17] and Vermeersch-Creusen[18] deny that the excommunication is incurred by simulated consent, on the grounds that he who feigns consent does not attempt to enter a matrimonial contract. Cerato,[19] however, rightly adverts to the fact that if consent were feigned it would nevertheless be presumed true in the external forum,[20] and hence the excommunication will be presumed in the external forum, even though it was not contracted. It is known that the plea to have the excommunication lifted on the grounds that a priest only feigned consent at a "mock wedding" was refused; but the penalty under such circumstances would seem to be a vindictive one, since if it were a censure, it should be lifted when the culprit is truly penitent, and has either repaired any damage caused or at least is prepared to do so.[21] Since canon 2388 decrees the penalty only for those who "dare" to break the law, the excuses enumerated in can. 2229, §2, viz., any diminution of imputability, excuse from the censure. Finally "the absolution from the censure aforesaid is so reserved to the Sacred Penitentiary that no one, except in the case of danger of death, can ever absolve from it, notwithstanding any faculty granted either by canon 2254, §1, or by privilege, or finally by any law whatsoever."[22]

---

[15] S. C. S. Off., 13 ian. 1892, ad 5—*Fontes,* n. 1147.

[16] *De Delictis et Poenis* (Romae, 1920), p. 390.

[17] *Tractatus Canonico-Moralis de Censuris iuxta C. I. C.* (3 ed., Romae: Marietti, 1933), n. 355, p. 308.

[18] *Epitome,* III, n. 592, pp. 368, 369.

[19] *Censurae Vigentes ipso facto a C. I. C. Excerptae* (2 ed., Patavii, 1921), n. 64, p. 308.

[20] C. 1086, §1.

[21] Cc. 2248, §1, §2; Can. 2242, §3.

[22] S. Poenit. declar., 4 maii 1937—*AAS,* XXIX (1937), 283 sqq.; Bouscaren, *The Canon Law Digest,* Suppl., pp. 203, 204.

A common law marriage likewise forms the basis for the incurring of the irregularity *from crime (irregularitas ex delicto)* mentioned in canon 985, 3°. This canon declares that if a person, who is already bound by a valid marriage bond, or by sacred orders, or by even simple and temporary religious vows, dares to attempt a marriage, he incurs an irregularity *from crime;* likewise a man, who dares to attempt marriage with a woman bound by a valid marriage bond or by even simple and temporary religious vows, incurs this irregularity.

Inasmuch as a religious who attempts marriage is considered in the law as automatically and legitimately dismissed from religion, a common law marriage attempted by the religious suffices as a basis for the incurring of such dismissal.[23]

Finally, any cleric who holds an ecclesiastical office is considered by the law to tacitly renounce that office if he attempts marriage.[24] Any office then, which is held by a cleric, is automatically vacant in the eyes of the law, if a common law marriage is attempted by the clerical incumbent in the office.

---

[23] C. 646, §1, 3°.

[24] C. 188, 5°.

CONCLUSIONS

1. The common law of marriage was Catholic in its origin and for three hundred years remained under Catholic administration.

2. "*Concubinatus*" as permitted in the early Church was not the sinful union condemned by the Council of Trent, but it was a real marriage.

3. Those exempted from observing the Catholic form of marriage decreed in canon 1094 do not have to observe the extraordinary form of marriage indicated in canon 1098.

4. Baptized non-Catholics may validly enter a common law marriage even when civil law forbids and does not recognize such unions.

5. For unbaptized persons marrying among themselves civil authority may decree diriment impediments and invalidating laws.

6. If even one party to a common law marriage be baptized, then the Church alone is competent to legislate for, and to adjudicate the marriage, except in its merely civil effects.

7. Baptized non-Catholics cannot enter common law marriage when not in each other's presence, except through the use of a procurator; unbaptized persons can contract common law marriage through correspondence.

8. A common law marriage can be proved to exist by the sworn oral testimony of the parties themselves, if no prejudice exists to a third party.

9. A common law marriage in which at least one party is a Catholic enjoys no presumption of validity unless it is recorded in an ecclesiastical register; a common law marriage of baptized non-Catholics enjoys the presumption of validity.

10. Clerics in sacred Orders and professed religious who attempt a common law marriage incur the penalties of canon 2388. Likewise, an attempted common law marriage incurs for clerics the penalty of canon 188, 5°; for religious the penalty of canon 646, §1, 3°; and for men whether clerics or laymen the penalty of canon 985, 3° (though these last three canons decree penalties only in the wide sense of the word).

BIBLIOGRAPHY

SOURCES

Acta Apostolicae Sedis, Commentarium Officiale, Romae, 1909– .

Acta et Decreta Concilii Plenarii Baltimorensis Tertii, Baltimorae, 1886.

Acta Sanctae Sedis, 41 vols., Romae, 1865–1908.

Bail, M. Ludovicus, *Summa Conciliorum,* 2 vols., Patavii, 1723.

Bullarium Ssmi. Domini nostri Benedicti XIV, 4 ed., 4 vols., Venetiis, 1878.

Bullarium Pontificium Sacrae Congregationis De Propaganda Fide, 7 vols. et index, Romae, 1839–1868.

Canones et Decreta Sacrosancti Oecumenici Concilii Tridentini sub Paulo III, Iulio III, et Pio IV Pontificibus Maximis, editio stereotypa, Ratisbonae, 1903.

Canons and Decrees of the Sacred and Oecumenical Council of Trent, The, translated by Waterworth, J., New York and London, 1848.

Codex Iuris Canonici Pii X Pontificis Maximi iussu digestus Benedicti Papae XV auctoritate promulgatus, Romae: Typis Polyglottis Vaticanis, 1917.

Codicis Iuris Canonici Fontes cura Emi. Petri Card. Gasparri Editi, 9 vols., Romae (postea Civitate Vaticana): Typis Polyglottis Vaticanis, 1923–39. (Vols. VII, VIII, IX ed. cura et studio Emi. Iustiniani Card. Serédi.)

Collectanea S. Congregationis de Propaganda Fide, 2 vols., Romae, 1907.

Collectio Librorum Iuris Anteiustiniani, 3 vols. in 2, ed. Krueger, Mommsen, Studemund, Berolini, 1890.

Concilii Tridentini Diariorum, Actorum, Epistolarum Tractatuum Nova Collectio, ed. Societas Gorresiana, 13 vols., Friburgi Brisgoviae: B. Herder, 1901–38.

Corpus Iuris Canonici, Editio Lipsiensis II post Aemilii Ludovici Richteri curas instruxit Aemilius Friedberg, 1879–1881. Editio anastatice repetita, Lipsiae: Tauchnitz, 1922.

Corpus Iuris Civilis, 3 vols., Berolini, 1928–29. *Institutiones,* quas recognovit P. Krueger; *Digesta,* quas recognovit T. Mommsen et retractavit P. Krueger; *Codex Iustinianus,* quem recognovit et retractavit P. Krueger; *Novellae,* quas recognovit R. Schoell, et absolvit G. Kroll.

Corpus Scriptorum Ecclesiasticorum Latinorum, 68 vols., Vindobonae, 1866–1936.

Denzinger, Henricus, *Enchiridion Symbolorum, Definitionum, et Declarationum De Rebus Fidei et Morum,* quod a Cl. Bannwart denuo compositum iteratis curis ed. Iohannes Bapt. Umberg, ed. 18–20, Friburgi Brisgoviae: Herder & Co., 1932.

HARDOUIN, JEAN, *Acta Conciliorum et Epistolae Decretales ac Constitutiones Summorum Pontificium*, 12 vols., Parisiis, 1715.

JAFFÉ, PH., *Regesta Pontificum Romanorum*, ed. secundam correctam et auctam auspiciis Guilelmi Wattenbach curaverunt F. Kaltenbrunner (ad annum 590), P. Ewald (anno 590–882), S. Löwenfeld (anno 882–1198), Lipsiae, 1885–1888.

Great Encyclical Letters of Pope Leo XIII, The, New York, Cincinnati, Chicago, 1903.

Ius Pontificium de Propaganda Fide, ed. R. deMartinis, pars I, 7 vols., Romae, 1888–98, pars II, Romae, 1909.

MANSI, JOANNES, *Sacrorum Conciliorum Nova et Amplissima Collectio*, 53 vols. in 59, Parisiis, 1901–27.

MIGNE, JACQUES PAUL, *Patrologiae Cursus Completus, Series Graeca*, 162 vols., Parisiis, 1857–66.

————, *Patrologiae Cursus Completus, Series Latina*, 221 vols., Parisiis, 1844–64.

Monumenta Germaniae Historica, Epistolae, ed. Societas Aperiendis Fontibus Rerum Germanicarum Medii Aevi, 8 vols., Vol. VIII (Karolini Aevi, VI), Berolini: Weidmanns, 1939.

————, *Leges*, ed. Societas Aperiendis Fontibus Rerum Germanicarum Medii Aevi, 5 vols., Lipsiae, 1925.

PITRA, I. B., *Iuris Ecclesiastici Graecorum Historia et Monumenta*, 2 vols., Romae, 1864–1868.

POTTHAST, A., *Regesta Pontificum*, 2 vols. in 1, Berolini, 1874–75.

Sacrae Romanae Rotae Decisiones seu Sententiae quae . . . prodierunt anno 1909– , Romae: Typis Vaticanis, 1912– .

Synodus Diocesana Fargensis Prima, Milwauchiae: Ex typographia Bruce, 1941.

WILKINS, D., *Concilia Magnae Brittaniae et Hiberniae*, 4 vols., Londini, 1737.

REFERENCE WORKS

Acta Congressus Iuridici Internationalis, 5 vols., Romae: Apud Custodiam Librariam Pont. Instituti Utriusque Iuris, 1935–1937.

AICHNER, SIMON, *Compendium Iuris Ecclesiastici*, 6 ed., Brixiniae, 1887.

ALFORD, CULVER BERNARD, *Jus Matrimoniale Comparatum*, New York: P. J. Kenedy & Sons, 1938.

ARTAUD, M. LE CHEVALIER, *Histoire du Pape Pie VII*, 2 vols., Louvain, 1836.

AYRINHAC, H. A.–LYDON, P. J., *Marriage Legislation in the New Code of Canon Law*, revised ed., New York: Benziger Brothers, 1932.

BALLINI, A. L., *Il Valore Giuridico della Celebrazione Nuziale Cristiana dal Primo Secolo all'Eta Giustinianea*, Pubblicazioni dell'universita Cattolica del S. Cuore: Serie Seconda, Scienze Giuridica, Vol. LXIV, Milano: Società Editrice—Vita e Pensiero, 1937.

BARONIUS, CAESAR, *Annales Ecclesiastici*, 37 vols., Vols. I–XXVIII, Barri-Ducis, 1864–1875, Vols. XXIX–XXXVII, Parisiis, 1876–1883.

BESTE, R. P. UDALRICUS, *Introductio in Codicem*, Collegeville, Minn.: St. John's Abbey Press, 1938.

BOUSCAREN, T. LINCOLN, *The Canon Law Digest*, 2 vols., and Supplement –1941, Milwaukee: The Bruce Publishing Company, 1934–1941.

BUCKLAND, W. W. and MCNAIR, ARNOLD D., *Roman Law and Common Law*, London: Cambridge Univ. Press, 1936.

CAPPELLO, FELIX M., *Tractatus Canonico-Moralis de Sacramentis*, Vol. III, *De Matrimonio*, ed. quarta emendata et aucta, Romae: apud Aedes Univ. Gregorianae, 1939.

————, *Tractatus Canonico-Moralis de Censuris iuxta C. I. C.*, 3 ed., Romae: Marietti, 1933.

CARBERRY, JOHN J., *The Juridical Form of Marriage*, The Catholic University of America Canon Law Studies, n. 84, Washington, D. C.: The Catholic University of America, 1934.

CATHREIN, VICTOR, *Philosophia Moralis*, ed. decima quinta, *Cursus Philosophicus*, pars VI, Friburgi Brisgoviae: Herder & Co., 1929.

CERATO, P., *Censurae Vigentes ipso facto a C. I. C. Excerptae*, 2 ed., Patavii, 1921.

CHELODI, IOANNES, *Ius Matrimoniale*, ed. quarta, recognita et aucta a V. Dalpiaz, Tridenti: Libreria Moderna Editrice A. Ardesi, 1937.

CICOGNANI, AMLETO, *Canon Law*, 2nd revised edition, authorized English version by Jos. O'Hara and Francis Brennan, Philadelphia: The Dolphin Press, 1935.

COCCHI, GUIDUS, *Commentarium in Codicem Iuris Canonici*, 5 vols. in 8, Vol. VIII, *De Delictis et Poenis*, 4 ed., Taurini: Marietti, 1938.

CORONATA, MATTHAEUS CONTE A, *Institutiones Iuris Canonici*, 5 vols., Taurini (Italia): Marietti, 1933–1939; Vols. I–II, 2 ed., 1939; Vol. III, 1933; Vol. IV, 1935; Vol. V, 1936.

COSCI, CHRISTOPHORUS, *De Sponsalibus Filiorumfamilias*, Romae, 1746.

CUJACIUS, JACOBUS, *In Lib. XII Resp. Aemilii Papiani*, Prati, 1837.

DEBECKER, IULIUS, *De Matrimonio Praelectiones Canonicae*, ed. nova, Louvain: Fr. Ceutrick, 1931.

DEPEY, *De l'autorité des deux puissances*, 4 vols., Strasbourg, 1788.

DESMET, AL., *Betrothment and Marriage*, trans. from the French edition of 1912 by W. Dobell, 2 vols. in 1, St. Louis, Mo., 1912.

————, *Tractatus Theologico-Canonicus De Sponsalibus et Matrimonio*, ed. quarta (inde a Codice altera), Brugis: Car. Beyaert, 1927.

DOHENY, WILLIAM J., *Canonical Procedure in Matrimonial Cases*, Milwaukee: The Bruce Publishing Company, 1938.

DUSKIE, JOHN A., *The Canonical Status of the Orientals in the United States*, The Catholic University of America Canon Law Studies, n. 48, Washington, D. C.: The Catholic University of America, 1928.

FEIJE, HENRICUS JOANNES, *De Impedimentis et Dispensationibus Matrimonialibus*, ed. secunda, Lovanii, 1874.

FREISEN, JOSEPH, *Geschichte des canonischen Eherechts bis zum Verfall der Glossenlitteratur,* 2 ed., Paderborn, 1893.

GASPARRI, PETRUS CARD., *Tractatus Canonicus De Matrimonio,* ed. nova ad mentem C. I. C. (Civitate Vaticana): Typis Polyglottis Vaticanis, 1932.

GIOVINE, PETRUS, *De Dispensationibus Matrimonialibus,* 2 vols., Neapoli, 1863–1866.

GRANDCLAUDE, E., *Jus Canonicum,* 3 vols., Parisiis, 1882–3.

JOYCE, GEO. HAYWARD, *Christian Marriage: An Historical and Doctrinal Study,* Heythrop Series: I, London and New York: Sheed and Ward, 1933.

KAY, THOMAS HENRY, *Competence in Matrimonial Procedure,* The Catholic University of America Canon Law Studies, n. 53, Washington, D. C.: The Catholic University of America, 1929.

KOEGEL, OTTO E., *Common Law Marriage and Its Development in the United States,* Washington: John Byrne & Co., 1922.

LEGA, MICHAËLIS CARD., *De Iudiciis Ecclesiasticis,* 2 ed., 2 vols., Romae: Ex Typographia Polyglotta, 1905.

LEGA, MICHAËLIS CARD. et BARTOCCETTI, VICTORIO, *Commentarius in Iudicia Ecclesiastica iuxta Codicem Iuris Canonici,* 3 vols., Romae: Anonima Libraria Cattolica Italiana, 1938–1941.

LIBERATORE, M., *Institutiones Philosophicae,* Vol. III, *Ethica et ius naturae,* 8 ed., Romae, 1855.

LINNEBORN, J., "*Grundriss des Eherechts nach dem Codex Iuris Canonici,* 5 ed., Paderborn: Ferdinand Schöningh, 1933.

MADDEN, J. W., *A Handbook of the Law of Persons and Domestic Relations,* 2 ed., St. Paul, Minn.: West Publishing Co., 1931.

MACKINTOSH, JAS., *Roman Law in Modern Practice,* Edinburgh: W. Green and Son, 1934.

MARTIN, J. P., *De Matrimonio ac potestate ipsum dirimendi ecclesiae soli exclusive propria,* 2 vols., Lugduni, 1844.

MARTINDALE-HUBBELL LAW DICTIONARY, 2 vols., 74 annual ed., Summitt, N. J.: Martindale Hubbell, Inc., 1942.

MAY, GEOFFREY, *Marriage Laws and Decisions in the United States,* New York: Russell Sage Foundation, 1929.

McCURDY, WM. EDW., *Cases on the Law of Persons and Domestic Relations,* 2 ed., National Case Book Series, Chicago: Callaghan and Co., 1933.

MUZZARELLI, ALPHONSE, *Il buon uso della logica in materia di religioni,* 11 vols. in 6, Firenze, 1821–1823.

NAU, LOUIS J., *Manual on the Marriage Laws of the Code of Canon Law,* 2 ed., New York and Cincinnati: Frederick Pustet Co., Inc., 1934.

O'BRIEN, JOHN P., *Common Law Marriage Status—Erlanger Opinion,* New York, 1932.

O'ROURKE, JAMES J., *Parish Registers,* The Catholic University of America Canon Law Studies, n. 88, Washington, D. C.: The Catholic University of America, 1934.

OTTAVIANI, ALAPHRIDUS, *Institutiones Iuris Publici Ecclesiastici,* 2 vols., ed. altera, Civitate Vaticana: Typis Polyglottis Vaticanis, 1935–36.

PANORMITANUS, ABBAS (Nicolaus de Tudeschis), *Commentaria in Quinque Libros Decretalium,* 5 vols. in 7, Venetiis, 1588.

PAYEN, G., *De Matrimonio in Missionibus et Potissimum in Sinis Tractatus Practicus et Casus,* 2 ed., 3 vols., Zi-ka-wei: In typographia T'ou-sè-wè, 1935–36.

PERRONE, IOANNES, *De Matrimonio Christiano,* 3 vols., Romae, 1858.

Petri Lombardi Libri IV Sententiarum, 2 ed., 2 vols., ad Claras Aquas: ex typographis collegii S. Bonaventurae, 1916.

POLLOCK, FR. and MAITLAND, FR. WM., *History of English Law,* 2 vols., Boston: Little, Brown & Co., 1931.

Pope and the People, The, London and Leamington, 1895.

QUIGLEY, JOSEPH, *Matrimonial Impediments and Dispensations,* Philadelphia: The Dolphin Press, 1939.

ROBERTI, F., *De Processibus,* 2 vols. in 1, Romae: Apud Aedes Facultatis Iuridicae ad S. Apollinaris, 1926.

ROSKOVÁNY, A. DE, *Matrimonium in Ecclesia Catholica,* 4 vols., Pestini (Nitriae), 1861–1881.

ROSSI, JOS., *De Matrimonii Celebratione iuxta C. I. C.,* Romae: F. Pustet, 1924.

SABETTI, ALOYSIUS et BARRETT, TIMOTHEUS, *Compendium Theologiae Moralis,* ed. tricesima tertia, Neo Eboraci, Cincinnati: Frederick Pustet Co., Inc., 1931.

SANCHEZ, THOMAS, *De Sancto Matrimonio Disputationum Libri Decem, in Tres Tomos Distributi,* Venetiis, 1712.

SARTORI, P. COSMAS, *Enchiridion Canonicum,* edit. VI, Vicetiae: Ex Typographia Commerciali, 1938.

SCHENCK, FRANCIS J., *The Matrimonial Impediments of Mixed Religion and Disparity of Cult,* The Catholic University of America Canon Law Studies, n. 51, Washington, D. C.: The Catholic University of America, 1929.

SCHMALZGRUEBER, FRANCISCUS, *Ius Ecclesiasticum Universum,* 5 vols. in 12, Romae, 1843–1845.

SCHOULER, JAMES, *A Treatise on the Law of Husband and Wife,* Boston, 1882.

SMITH, WALTER DENTON, *A Handbook of Elementary Law,* Hornbook Series, 2 ed., St. Paul, Minn.: West Publishing Co., 1939.

THOMAS AQUINAS, *S. Thomae Aquinatis Doctoris Angelici Summa Theologica,* 6 vols., Augustae Taurinorum: Typographia Pontificia, 1903.

VEERMEERSCH, A.-CREUSEN, J., *Epitome Iuris Canonici,* 3 vols., Vol. I, 6 ed., 1937; Vols. II–III, 5 ed., 1936, Mechliniae–Romae: H. Dessain.

VLAMING, *Praelectiones Iuris Matrimonii,* 3 ed., 2 vols., Bussum in Hollandia, Vol. I, 1919; Vol. II, 1921.

VROMANT, G., *Ius Missionariorum,* Vol. V, *De Matrimonio,* Louvain: Museum Lessianum, 1931.

WANENMACHER, FRANCIS, *Canonical Evidence in Marriage Cases,* Philadelphia, Pa.: Dolphin Press, 1935.

WERNZ, FRANCISCUS X., *Ius Decretalium,* 6 vols., Vol IV, *Ius Matrimoniale Ecclesiae Catholicae,* Romae, 1904.

WERNZ-VIDAL, *Ius Canonicum,* 7 vols. in 8, Vol. V, *De Matrimonio,* 2 ed., Romae: apud Aedes Universitatis Gregorianae, 1928.

WHALEN, DONALD, *The Value of Testimonial Evidence in Matrimonial Procedure,* The Catholic University of America Canon Law Studies, n. 99, Washington, D. C.: The Catholic University of America, 1935.

WOYWOD, STANISLAUS, *The New Canon Law,* New York, 1918.

PERIODICALS

Analecta Ecclesiastica, Romae, 1893–1911.

Apollinaris, Romae, 1928– .

Archiv für katholisches Kirchenrecht, Innsbruck, 1857–1861; Mainz, 1862– .

Canoniste Contemporain, Le, Paris, 1878–1926.

Ephemerides Theologicae Lovanienses, Lovanii, 1924– .

Monitore Ecclesiastico, Il, Romae, 1876– .

Jurist, The, Washington, D. C., 1941– .

Ius Pontificium, Romae, 1921– .

Periodica de Re Canonica et Morali utili Praesertim Religiosis et Missionariis, Bruges, 1905– .

University of Chicago Law Review, 1933– .

ARTICLES

DALPIAZ, V., "An in altera instantia causae de qua in can. 1971, §1, n. 2, requiratur ad validitatem interventus promotoris iustitiae, etiamsi defensor vinculi appellationem interposuerit?"—*Apollinaris,* VIII (1935), 139–140.

GRENTRUP, J., "Die Rassenmischehen in den deutschen Kolonien und das kanonische Recht."—*AKKR,* XCIV (1914), 1–34.

GRANDCLAUDE, E., "Competence de l'État Touchant le Mariage des Infideles."—*Canoniste Contemporain, Le,* X (1887), 241–257.

HANNAN, JEROME D., "Automatic Sanation of Marriage."—*The Jurist,* I (1941), 146–149.

HILLING, N., "Neueste Entscheidungen des Hl. Stuhles über das Ehehindernis der Religionsverschiedenheit, die Auflösung einer Naturehe und die Anwendung des Privilegium Paulinum."—*AKKR,* CVII (1927), 178–186.

———, "Kanonistiches Gutachten über das Verbot der Rassenmischehen in den deutschen Kolonien."—*AKKR,* XCV (1915), 683–690.

ONCLIN, W., "De regimine Matrimonii Fidelem inter et Infidelem."—*Ephemerides Theologicae Lovanienses,* X (1933), 47–62.

POUND, ROSCOE, "What Is the Common Law?"—Univ. of Chicago Law Review, IV (1936–1937), 176–189.

LIST OF ABBREVIATIONS

AAS—*Acta Apostolicae Sedis.*
ASS—*Acta Sanctae Sedis.*
AKKR—*Archiv für katholisches Kirchenrecht.*
Cod.—Codex Iustinianus.
Coll. Lac.—*Acta et Decreta Sacrorum Conciliorum Recentiorum, Collectio Lacensis.*
CSEL—*Corpus Scriptorum Ecclesiasticorum Latinorum.*
D—*Digstrum Iustinianum.*
ETL—*Ephemerides Theologicae Lovanienses.*
Fontes—*Codicis Iuris Canonici Fontes cura . . . Gasparri editi.*
JE, JK, JL—*Regesta Pontificum Romanorum.*
Mansi—*Sacrorum Conciliorum Nova et Amplissima Collectio.*
MPG—*Patrologiae Cursus Completus, Series Graeca.*
MPL—*Patrologiae Cursus Completus, Series Latina.*
Nov.—*Novellae Iustinianae.*
PCI—*Pontificia Commissio Interpretationis.*

BIOGRAPHICAL NOTE

Robert Edward Dillon was born February 4, 1911, in Binghamton, New York. He received his elementary and high school education at St. Patrick's Academy, Binghamton, his college education at Holy Cross College, Worcester, Mass. After receiving the Bachelor of Arts degree from the latter institution in 1932, he pursued a course in theology at St. Bernard's Seminary, Rochester, N. Y. On June 6, 1936, he was ordained to the priesthood. After three years of parochial work in the Diocese of Syracuse, New York, he enrolled, in September, 1939, in the school of Canon Law at the Catholic University of America, where he received the degree of the Baccalaureate in Canon Law in June, 1940, and the degree of the Licentiate in Canon Law in June, 1941.

ALPHABETICAL INDEX

CANON LAW STUDIES

1. Freriks, Rev. Celestine A., C.PP.S., J.C.D., Religious Congregations in Their External Relations, 121 pp., 1916.
2. Galliher, Rev. Daniel M., O.P., J.C.D., Canonical Elections, 117 pp., 1917.
3. Borowski, Rev. Aurelius L., O.F.M., J.C.D., De Confraternitatibus Ecclesiasticis, 136 pp., 1918.
4. Castillo, Rev. Cayo, J.C.D., Disertacion Historico-Canonica sobre la Potestad del Cabildo en Sede Vacante o Impedida del Vicario Capitular, 99 pp., 1919 (1918).
5. Kubelbeck, Rev. William J., S.T.B., J.C.D., The Sacred Penitentiaria and Its Relations to Faculties of Ordinaries and Priests, 129 pp., 1918.
6. Petrovits, Rev. Joseph J. C., S.T.D., J.C.D., The New Church Law On Matrimony, X-461 pp., 1919.
7. Hickey, Rev. John J., S.T.B., J.C.D., Irregularities and Simple Impediments in the New Code of Canon Law, 100 pp., 1920.
8. Klekotka, Rev. Peter J., S.T.B., J.C.D., Diocesan Consultors, 179 pp., 1920.
9. Wanenmacher, Rev. Francis, J.C.D., The Evidence in Ecclesiastical Procedure Affecting the Marriage Bond, 1920 (Printed 1935).
10. Golden, Rev. Henry Francis, J.C.D., Parochial Benefices in the New Code, IV–119 pp., 1921 (Printed 1925).
11. Koudelka, Rev. Charles J., J.C.D., Pastors, Their Rights and Duties According to the New Code of Canon Law, 211 pp., 1921.
12. Melo, Rev. Antonius, O.F.M., J.C.D., De Exemptione Regularium, X–188 pp., 1921.
13. Schaaf, Rev. Valentine Theodore, O.F.M., S.T.B., J.C.D., The Cloister, X–180 pp., 1921.
14. Burke, Rev. Thomas Joseph, S.T.D., J.C.D., Competence in Ecclesiastical Tribunals, IV–117 pp., 1922.
15. Leech, Rev. George Leo, J.C.D., A Comparative Study of the Constitution, "Apostolicae Sedis" and the "Codex Juris Canonici," 179 pp., 1922.
16. Motry, Rev. Hubert Louis, S.T.D., J.C.D., Diocesan Faculties According to the Code of Canon Law, II–167 pp., 1922.
17. Murphy, Rev. George Lawrence, J.C.D., Delinquencies and Penalties in the Administration and Reception of the Sacraments, IV–121 pp., 1923.
18. O'Reilly, Rev. John Anthony, S.T.B., J.C.D., Ecclesiastical Sepulture in the New Code of Canon Law, II–129 pp., 1923.

19. Michalicka, Rev. Wenceslas Cyrill, O.S.B., J.C.D., Judicial Procedure in Dismissal of Clerical Exempt Religious, 107 pp., 1923.
20. Dargin, Rev. Edward Vincent, S.T.B., J.C.D., Reserved Cases According to the Code of Canon Law, IV–103 pp., 124.
21. Godfrey, Rev. John A., S.T.B., J.C.D., The Right of Patronage According to the Code of Canon Law, 153 pp., 1924.
22. Hagedorn, Rev. Francis Edward, J.C.D., General Legislation on Indulgences, II–154 pp., 1924.
23. King, Rev. James Ignatius, J.C.D., The Administration of the Sacraments to Dying Non-Catholics, V–141 pp., 1924.
24. Winslow, Rev. Francis Joseph, A.F.M., J.C.D., Vicars and Prefects Apostolic, IV–149 pp., 1924.
25. Correa, Rev. Jose Servelion, S.T.D., J.C.D., La Potestad Legislativa de la Iglesia Catolica, IV–127 pp., 1925.
26. Dugan, Rev. Henry Francis, A.M., J.C.D., The Judiciary Department of the Diocesan Curia, 87 pp., 1925.
27. Keller, Rev. Charles Frederick, S.T.B., J.C.D., Mass Stipends, 167 pp., 1925.
28. Paschang, Rev. John Linus, J.C.D., The Sacramentals According to the Code of Canon Law, 129 pp., 1925.
29. Pointek, Rev. Cyrillus, O.F.M., S.T.B., J.C.D., De Indulto Exclaustrationis necnon Saecularizationis, XIII–289 pp., 1925.
30. Kearney, Rev. Richard Joseph, S.T.B., J.C.D., Sponsors at Baptism According to the Code of Canon Law, IV–127 pp., 1925.
31. Bartlett, Rev. Chester Joseph, A.M., LL.B., J.C.D., The Tenure of Parochial Property in the United States of America, V–108 pp., 1926.
32. Kilker, Rev. Adrian Jerome, J.C.D., Extreme Unction, V–425 pp., 1926.
33. McCormick, Rev. Robert Emmett, J.C.D., Confessors of Religious, VIII–266 pp., 1926.
34. Miller, Rev. Newton Thomas, J.C.D., Founded Masses According to the Code of Canon Law, VII–93 pp., 1926.
35. Roelker, Rev. Edward G., S.T.D., J.C.D., Principles of Privilege According to the Code of Canon Law, XI–166 pp., 1926.
36. Bakalarczyk, Rev. Richardus, M.I.C., J.U.D., De Novitiatu, VIII–208 pp., 1927
37. Pizzuti, Rev. Lawrence, O.F.M., J.U.L., De Parochis Religiosis, 1927. (Not printed.)
38. Bliley, Rev. Nicholas Martin, O.S.B., J.C.D., Altars According to the Code of Canon Law, XIX–132 pp., 1927.
39. Brown, Mr. Brendan Francis, A.B., LL.M., J.U.D., The Canonical Juristic Personality with Special Reference to Its Status in the United States of America, V–212 pp., 1927.
40. Cavanaugh, Rev. William Thomas, C.P., J.U.D., The Reservation of the Blessed Sacrament, VIII-101 pp., 1927.

41. Doheny, Rev. William J., C.S.C., A.B., J.U.D., Church Property: Modes of Acquisition, X–118 pp., 1927.
42. Feldhaus, Rev. Aloysius H., C.PP.S., J.C.D., Oratories, IX–141 pp., 1927.
43. Kelly, Rev. James Patrick, A.B., J.C.D., The Jurisdiction of the Simple Confessor, X–208 pp., 1927.
44. Neuberger, Rev. Nicholas J., J.C.D., Canon 6 or the Relation of the Codex Juris Canonici to the Preceding Legislation, V-95 pp., 1927.
45. O'Keefe, Rev. Gerald Michael, J.C.D., Matrimonial Dispensations, Powers of Bishops, Priests and Confessors, VIII–232 pp., 1927.
46. Quigley, Rev. Joseph, A.M., A.B., J.C.B., Condemned Societies, 139 pp., 1927.
47. Zaplotnik, Rev. Johannes Leo, J.C.D., De Vicariis Foraneis, X–142 pp., 1927.
48. Duskie, Rev. John Aloysius, A.B., J.C.D., The Canonical Status of the Orientals in the United States, VIII–196 pp., 1928.
49. Hyland, Rev. Francis Edward, J.C.D., Excommunication, Its Nature, Historical Development and Effects, VIII–181 pp., 1928.
50. Reinmann, Rev. Gerald Joseph, O.M.C., J.C.D., The Third Order Secular of Saint Francis, 201 pp., 1928.
51. Schenk, Rev. Francis J., J.C.D., The Matrimonial Impediments of Mixed Religion and Disparity of Cult, XVI–318 pp., 1929.
52. Coady, Rev. John Joseph, S.T.D., J.U.D., A.M., The Appointment of Pastors, VIII–150 pp., 1929.
53. Kay, Rev. Thomas Henry, J.C.D., Competence in Matrimonial Procedure, VIII–164 pp., 1929.
54. Turner, Rev. Sidney Joseph, C.P., J.U.D., The Vow of Poverty, XLIX–217 pp., 1929.
55. Kearney, Rev. Raymond A., A.B., S.T.D., J.C.D., The Principles of Delegation, VII–149 pp., 1929.
56. Conran, Rev. Edward James, A.B., J.C.D., The Interdict, V–163 pp., 1930.
57. O'Neil, Rev. William H., J.C.D., Papal Rescripts of Favor, VII–218 pp., 1930.
58. Bastnagel, Rev. Clement Vincent, J.U.D., The Appointment of Parochial Adjutants and Assistants, XV–257 pp., 1930.
59. Ferry, Rev. William A., A.B., J.C.D., Stole Fees, V–135 pp., 1930.
60. Costello, Rev. John Michael, A.B., J.C.D., Domicile and Quasi-domicile, VII–201 pp., 1930.
61. Kremer, Rev. Michael Nicholas, A.B., S.T.B., J.C.D., Church Support in the United States, VI–1930.
62. Angulo, Rev. Luis, C.M., J.C.D., Legislation de la Iglesia sobre la intencion en la application de la Santa Misa, VII–104 pp., 1931.
63. Frey, Rev. Wolfgang Norbert, O.S.B., A.B., J.C.D., The Act of Religious Profession, VIII–174 pp., 1931.

64. Roberts, Rev. James Brendan, A.B., J.C.D., The Banns of Marriage, XIV–140 pp., 1931.
65. Ryder, Rev. Raymond Aloysius, A.B., J.C.D., Simony, IX–151 pp., 1931.
66. Campagna, Rev. Angelo, Ph.D., J.U.D., Il Vicario Generale del Vescovo, VII–205 pp., 1931.
67. Cox, Rev. Joseph Godfrey, A.B., J.C.D., The Administration of Seminaries, VI–124 pp., 1931.
68. Gregory, Rev. Donald J., J.U.D., The Pauline Privilege, XV–165 pp., 1931.
69. Donohue, Rev. John F., J.C.D., The Impediment of Crime, VII–110 pp., 1931.
70. Dooley, Rev. Eugene A., O.M.I., J.C.D., Church Law on Sacred Relics, IX–143 pp., 1931.
71. Orth, Rev. Raymond Clement, O.M.C., J.C.D., The Approbation of Religious Institutes, 171 pp., 1931.
72. Pernicone, Rev. Joseph M., A.B., J.C.D., The Ecclesiastical Prohibition of Books, XII–267 pp., 1932.
73. Clinton, Rev. Connell, A.B., J.C.D., The Paschal Precept, IX–108 pp., 1932.
74. Donnelly, Rev. Francis B., A.M., S.T.L., J.C.D., The Diocesan Synod, VIII–125 pp., 1932.
75. Torrente, Rev. Camilo, C.M.F., J.C.D., Las Processiones Sagradas, V–145 pp., 1932.
76. Murphy, Rev. Edwin J., C.PP.S., J.C.D., Suspension Ex Informata Conscientia, XI–122 pp., 1932.
77. Mackenzie, Rev. Eric F., A.M., S.T.L., J.C.D., The Delict of Heresy in Its Commission, Penalization, Absolution, VII–124 pp., 1932.
78. Lyons, Rev. Avitus E., S.T.B., J.C.D., The Collegiate Tribunal of First Instance, XI–147 pp., 1932.
79. Connolly, Rev. Thomas A., J.C.D., Appeals, XI–195 pp., 1932.
80. Sangmeister, Rev. Joseph V., A.B., J.C.D., Force and Fear as Precluding Matrimonial Consent, V–211 pp., 1932.
81. Jaeger, Rev. Leo A., A.B., J.C.D., The Administration of Vacant and Quasi-vacant Episcopal Sees in the United States, IX–229 pp., 1932.
82. Rimlinger, Rev. Herbert T., J.C.D., Error Invalidating Matrimonial Consent, VII–79 pp., 1932.
83. Barrett, Rev. John, D.M., S.S., J.C.D., A Comparative Study of the Third Plenary Council of Baltimore and the Code, IX–221 pp., 1932.
84. Carberry, Rev. John J., Ph.D., S.T.D., J.C.D., The Juridical Form of Marriage, X–177 pp., 1934.
85. Dolan, Rev. John L., A.B., J.C.D., The Defensor Vinculi, XII–157 pp., 1934.
86. Hannan, Rev. Jerome D., A.M., S.T.D., LL.B., J.C.D., The Canon Law of Wills, IX–517 pp., 1934.

87. Lemieux, Rev. Delisle A., A.M., J.C.D., The Sentence in Ecclesiastical Procedure, IX–131 pp., 1934.
88. O'Rourke, Rev. James J., A.B., J.C.D., Parish Registers, VII–109 pp., 1934.
89. Timlin, Rev. Bartholomew, O.F.M., A.M., J.C.D., Conditional Matrimonial Consent, X–381 pp., 1934.
90. Wahl, Rev. Francis X., A.B., J.C.D., The Matrimonial Impediments of Consanguinity and Affinity, VI–125 pp., 1934.
91. White, Rev. Robert J., A.B., LL.B., S.T.B., J.C.D., Canonical Ante-Nuptial Promises and the Civil Law, VI–152 pp., 1934.
92. Herrera, Rev. Antonio Parra, O.C.D., J.C.D., Legislation Ecclesiastica sobra el Ayuno y la Abstinencia, XI–191 pp., 1935.
93. Kennedy, Rev. Edwin J., J.C.D., The Special Matrimonial Process in Cases of Evident Nullity, X–165 pp., 1935.
94. Manning, Rev. John J., A.B., J.C.D., Presumption of Law in Matrimonial Procedure, XI–111 pp., 1935.
95. Moeder, Rev. John M., J.C.D., The Proper Bishop for Ordination and Dismissorial Letters, VII–135 pp., 1935.
96. O'Mara, Rev. William A., A.B., J.C.D., Canonical Causes for Matrimonial Dispensations, IX–155 pp., 1935.
97. Reilly, Rev. Peter, J.C.D., Residence of Pastors, IX–81 pp., 1935.
98. Smith, Rev. Mariner T., O.P., S.T.L., J.C.D., The Penal Law for Religious, VII–169 pp., 1935.
99. Whalen, Rev. Donald W., A.M., J.C.D., The Value of Testimonial Evidence in Matrimonial Procedure, XIII–297 pp., 1935.
100. Cleary, Rev. Joseph F., J.C.D., Canonical Limitations on the Alienation of Church Property, VIII–141 pp., 1936.
101. Glynn, Rev. John C., J.C.D., The Promoter of Justice, XX–337 pp., 1936.
102. Brennan, Rev. James H., S.S., A.M., S.T.B., J.C.D., The Simple Convalidation of Marriage, VI–135 pp., 1937.
103. Brunini, Rev. Joseph Bernard, J.C.D., The Clerical Obligations of Canons 139 and 142, X–121 pp., 1937.
104. Connor, Rev. Maurice, A.B., J.C.D., The Administrative Removal of Pastors, VIII–159 pp., 1937.
105. Guilfoyle, Rev. Merlin Joseph, J.C.D., Custom, XI–144 pp., 1937.
106. Hughes, Rev. James Austin, A.B., A.M., J.C.D., Witnesses in Criminal Trials of Clerics, IX–140 pp., 1937.
107. Jansen, Rev. Raymond J., A.B., S.T.L., J.C.D., Canonical Provisions for Catechetical Instruction, VII–153 pp., 1937.
108. Kealy, Rev. John James, A.B., J.C.D., The Introductory Libellus in Church Court Procedure, XI–121 pp., 1937.
109. McManus, Rev. James Edward, C.SS.R., J.C.D., The Administration of Temporal Goods in Religious Institutes, XVI–196 pp., 1937.
110. Moriarity, Rev. Eugene James, J.C.D., Oaths in Ecclesiastical Courts, X–115 pp., 1937.

111. Rainer, Rev. Eligius George, C.SS.R., J.C.D., Suspension of Clerics, XVII–249 pp., 1937.
112. Reilly, Rev. Thomas F., C.SS.R., J.C.D., Visitation of Religious, VI–195 pp., 1938.
113. Moriarty, Rev. Francis E., C.SS.R., J.C.D., The Extraordinary Absolution from Censures, XV–334 pp., 1938.
114. Connolly, Rev. Nicholas P., J.C.D., The Canonical Erection of Parishes, X–132 pp., 1938.
115. Donovan, Rev. James Joseph, J.C.D., The Pastor's Obligation in Prenuptial Investigation, XII–322 pp., 1938.
116. Harrigan, Rev. Robert J., M.A., S.T.B., J.C.D., The Radical Sanation of Invalid Marriages, VIII–208 pp., 1938.
117. Boffa, Rev. Conrad Humbert, J.C.D., Canonical Provisions for Catholic Schools, X–211 pp., 1939.
118. Parsons, Rev. Anscar John, O.M. Cap., J.C.D., Canonical Elections, XII–236 pp., 1939.
119. Reilly, Rev. Edward Michael, A.B., J.C.D., The General Norms of Dispensation, X–156 pp., 1939.
120. Ryan, Rev. Gerald Aloysius, A.B., J.C.D., Principles of Episcopal Jurisdiction, XII–172 pp., 1939.
121. Burton, Rev. Francis James, C.S.C., A.B., J.C.D., A Commentary on Canon 1125, X–222 pp., 1940.
122. Miaskiewicz, Rev. Francis Sigismund, J.C.D., Supplied Jurisdiction According to Canon 209, XII–340 pp., 1940.
123. Rice, Rev. Patrick William, A.B., J.C.D., Proof of Death in Prenuptial Investigation, VIII–156 pp., 1940.
124. Anglin, Rev. Thomas Francis, M.S., J.C.D., The Eucharistic Fast, VIII–183 pp., 1941.
125. Coleman, Rev. John Jerome, J.C.L., The Minister of Confirmation, VI–153 pp., 1941.
126. Downs, Rev. John Emmanuel, A.B., J.C.D., The Concept of Clerical Immunity, XI–163 pp., 1941.
127. Esswein, Rev. Anthony Albert, J.C.D., Extrajudicial Penal Powers of Ecclesiastical Superiors, X–144 pp., 1941.
128. Farrel, Rev. Benjamin Francis, M.A., S.T.L., J.C.D., The Rights and Duties of the Local Ordinary Regarding Congregations of Women Religious of Pontifical Approval, V–195 pp., 1941.
129. Feeney, Rev. Thomas John, A.B., S.T.L., J.C.D., Restitutio in Integrum, VI–169 pp., 1941.
130. Findlay, Rev. Stephen William, O.S.B., A.B., J.C.D., Canonical Norms Governing the Deposition and Degradation of Clerics, XVII–279 pp., 1941.
131. Goodwine, Rev. John, A.B., S.T.L., J.C.L., The Right of the Church to Acquire Property, VIII–119 pp., 1941.
132. Heston, Rev. Edward Louis, C.S.C., Ph.D., S.T.D., J.C.D., The

Alienation of Church Property in the United States, XII–222 pp., 1941.

133. Hogan, Rev. James John, S.T.L., J.C.D., Judicial Advocates and Procurators, VIII–200 pp., 1941.
134. Kealy, Rev. Thomas M., A.B., Litt. B., J.C.D., Dowry of Women Religious, IX–152 pp., 1941.
135. Keene, Rev. Michael James, O.S.B., J.C.D., Religious Ordinaries and Canon 198, 1941.
136. Kerin, Rev. Charles A., S.S., M.A., S.T.B., J.C.D., The Privation of Christian Burial, XVI–279 pp., 1941.
137. Louis, Rev. William Francis, M.A., J.C.D., Diocesan Archives, X–109 pp., 1941.
138. McDevitt, Rev. Gilbert Joseph, A.B., J.C.D., Legitimacy and Legitimation, X–247 pp., 1941.
139. McDonough, Rev. Thomas Joseph, A.B., J.C.D., Apostolic Administrators, X–217 pp., 1941
140. Meier, Rev. Carl Anthony, A.B., J.C.D., Penal Administrative Procedure Against Negligent Pastors, XI–240 pp., 1941.
141. Schmidt, Rev. John Rogg, A.B., J.C.D., The Principles of Authentic Interpretation in Canon 17 of the Code of Canon Law, XII–331 pp., 1941.
142. Slafkosky, Rev. Andrew Leonard, A.B., J.C.D., The Canonical Episcopal Visitation of the Diocese, X–197 pp., 1941.
143. Swoboda, Rev. Innocent Robert, O.F.M., J.C.D., Ignorance in Relation to the Imputability of Delicts, IX–271 pp., 1941.
144. Dubé, Rev. Arthur Joseph, A.B., J.C.D., The General Principles for the Reckoning of Time in Canon Law, VIII–299 pp., 1941.
145. McBride, Rev. James T., A.B., J.C.D., Incardination and Excardination of Seculars, XX–585 pp., 1941.
146. Król, Rev. John J., J.C.L., The Defendant in Contentious Trials.
147. Comyns, Rev. Joseph J., C.SS.R., J.C.L., The Papal and Episcopal Administration of Church Property.
148. Barry, Rev. Garrett Francis, O.M.I., J.C.L., Violation of the Cloister.
149. Bolduc, Rev. Gatien, C.S.V., A.B., S.T.L., J.C.L., Les études dans les religions cléricales.
150. Boyle, Rev. David John, M.A., J.C.L., The Juridic Effects of Moral Certitude on Pre-Nuptial Guarantees.
151. Canavan, Rev. Walter Joseph, M.A., Litt.D., J.C.L., Profession of Faith.
152. Desrochers, Rev. Bruno, A.B., Ph.L., S.T.B., J.C.L., Le Premier Concile Plénier de Québec et le Code de Droit Canonique.
153. Dillon, Rev. Robert Edward, A.B., J.C.L., Common Law Marriage.
154. Dodwell, Rev. Edward John, Ph.D., S.T.B., J.C.L., The Time and Place for the Celebration of Marriage.
155. Donnellan, Rev. Thomas Andrew, A.B., J.C.L., The Obligation of the Missa pro Populo.

156. Eltz, Rev. Louis Anthony, A.B., J.C.L., Co-operation in Crime.
157. Gass, Rev. Sylvester Francis, M.A., J.C.L., Ecclesiastical Pensions.
158. Guiniven, Rev. John Joseph, C.SS.R., J.C.L., The Precept of Hearing Mass on Sundays and Holy Days of Obligation.
159. Gulczynski, Rev. John Theophilus, J.C.L., The Desecration and Violation of Churches.
160. Hammill, Rev. John Leo, M.A., J.C.L., The Obligations of the Traveler According to Canon 14.
161. Haydt, Rev. John Joseph, A.B., J.C.L., Reserved Benefices.
162. Huser, Rev. Roger John, O.F.M., A.B., J.C.L., The Crime of Abortion in Canon Law.
163. Kearney, Rev. Francis Patrick, A.B., S.T.L., J.C.L., The Principles of Canon 1127.
164. Linahen, Rev. Leo James, S.T.L., J.C.L., De Absolutione Complicis in Peccato Turpi.
165. McCloskey, Rev. Joseph Aloysius, A.B., J.C.L., The Subject of Ecclesiastical Law according to Canon 12.
166. O'Neill, Rev. Francis Joseph, C.SS.R., J.C.L., The Dismissal of Religious in Temporary Vows.
167. Prince, Rev. John Edward, A.B., S.T.B., J.C.L., The Diocesan Chancellor.
168. Riesner, Rev. Albert Joseph, C.SS.R., J.C.L., Apostates and Fugitives from Religious Institutes.
169. Stenger, Rev. Joseph Bernard, J.C.L., The Mortgaging of Church Property.
170. Waldron, Rev. Joseph Francis, A.B., J.C.L., The Minister of Baptism.
171. Willett, Rev. Robert Albert, J.C.L., The Probative Value of Documents in Ecclesiastical Trials.
172. Woeber, Rev. Edward Martin, M.A., J.C.L., The Interpellations.

www.ingramcontent.com/pod-product-compliance
Lightning Source LLC
LaVergne TN
LVHW050218080826
844660LV00012B/433